BOHEMIAN RHAPSODY

weldon**owen**

Published in North America by
Weldon Owen
1045 Sansome Street
San Francisco, CA 94111
www.weldonowen.com

First published in the UK in 2018 by Carlton Books Limited

Editorial Director: Roland Hall
Design: Russell Knowles
Production: Yael Steinitz

Library of Congress Cataloging in Publication data is available.

ISBN: 978-1-68188-467-7

10 9 8 7 6 5 4 3 2 1

Printed in Italy

BOHEMIAN RHAPSODY

THE INSIDE STORY

THE OFFICIAL BOOK OF THE FILM

weldonowen

CONTENTS

RIGHT: Rami Malek as Freddie Mercury in *Bohemian Rhapsody*.

FOREWORDS

This book is a souvenir of *Bohemian Rhapsody*, the movie, and a tribute to the actors who brought Freddie and his pals to new life, along with the costumiers, set designers, chippies, painters, lighting and sound men, cameramen, directors and supporting team who all gave far beyond the call of duty to complete this project to the max, through times that were often very demanding.

The film is the result of a long and uniquely challenging journey. Roger and myself, along with Jim Beach, our manager, in partnership with fearless independent film producer Graham King, took up the challenge of creating a movie that would tell the story honestly and engagingly, and above all do justice to the phenomenon that was our dear friend and colleague Freddie Mercury. From the decision to create a script around 2009, we spent eight years in development, and in the search for a director and film studio to take the film on. In the final stretch, after 20th Century Fox had committed, Roger and I stepped back and watched an amazing team swing into action; while we toured the arenas of the world once again, they filmed an epic.

For us it was an enormous leap of faith; we realised we were about to watch actors depict US on the screen – who in the world is fortunate enough to see that happen? But it was also, of course, a daunting prospect. Once the cast was assembled, we were able to spend time with them, and get to know them, and also to communicate something of ourselves and our ways to help them paint the picture. The actors, led by Rami Malek as Freddie, quickly turned out to be such an extraordinarily talented and devoted team that we actually relaxed, and felt our legacy was in safe hands! We all learned that a film like *Bohemian Rhapsody* is not a documentary, but a depiction which seeks to delineate a symbolic truth – something like a painting or a historical novel. In the process of 'becoming us', the leading actors, with our full blessing, actually improvised much of what you see – under the directorship of first Brian Singer, and then Dexter Fletcher.

In the excellent photographs in this book, Alex Bailey has captured much of the atmosphere of the shoots, the stunningly real sets, and the chemistry of the interactions of the performances. These are precious moments, which we hope will endure as a lasting testament to the one and only Faroukh Bulsara, known to the world as Freddie Mercury.

BRIAN MAY, JULY 2018

Ditto……Enjoy!

ROGER TAYLOR, JULY 2018

VOX

BOHEMIAN RHAPSODY

CHAPTER ONE

A KIND OF MAGIC: FROM PAGE TO SCREEN

THE MIRACLE

How producer Graham King prepared to tell the Queen story

Oscar-winning producer Graham King was working on Martin Scorsese's film *Hugo* in 2010, when he got a call from the screenwriter Peter Morgan. He asked if King liked Queen. King said he did. And so Morgan confided that he was in the process of writing a speculative script about the band and Freddie Mercury, and thought King would be the ideal person to oversee its journey to the screen.

Having grown up in London in the 70s and 80s, King was familiar with some aspects of the narrative, but made sure he did plenty of homework before setting up a conversation with Queen's long-time manager Jim "Miami" Beach. That three-hour phone call led to a meeting in a London restaurant with Brian May and Roger Taylor. "They were keen on the idea," says King, "but also a little apprehensive, as anyone would be about someone else telling their life story."

King had previously produced the Howard Hughes biopic *The Aviator* with Scorsese, and *Ali* with Michael Mann (he later went on to executive produce the Oscar-winning film *Argo* with Ben Affleck), and persuaded the remaining active members of Queen that their history deserved to be told at that level. Duly convinced, they were heavily involved in the project from that moment on. "That was the way I wanted it," King says. "You can read books and articles and watch videos and interviews, but no one knows the story better than them. They can tell you things that you would never find out otherwise. It meant the world to me to have built this family between us all."

The jigsaw of the story wasn't easy to put together, and there were several stops and starts in the subsequent years of development. "I was very much of the mindset that we shouldn't make this unless we felt it was really right," King explains. "Storywise, castwise, everything had to fall into place." The narrative had to encompass Freddie's journey from shy, buck-toothed, Zanzibar-born immigrant child to stage-conquering, world-dominating rock star; his meeting the rest of Queen; the working relationship they forged to create their unique sound; and the layers of complexity making up Freddie's personal life, his sexuality and his contracting the HIV virus. It was not an easy balancing act.

All those elements, however, ended up in service to Queen's greatest achievement. "This film is a celebration of the music first and foremost," says King. "It's about carrying on Freddie and Queen's legacy: these songs that are larger-than-life, and put a smile on your face and bring people together. If you're at a sporting event anywhere in the world and you hear 'We Are the Champions', you can't help but clap and sing with the person next to you, no matter who they are. That's the feeling I wanted the film to capture. I felt that if we achieved that alongside the emotion of Freddie's story, then we'd have a film that all audiences could go and enjoy."

PREVIOUS PAGE: The four main actors recreate one of Queen's all-time great photographs.

ABOVE: Jacketed against the wind, Joseph Mazzello, Ben Hardy and Gwilym Lee prepare to recreate Live Aid at Hemel Hempstead.

BELOW: A pre-Live Aid rehearsal room huddle for the four actors.

LEFT: The scene in which the band celebrates landing a slot on *Top of the Pops*. (Queen replaced David Bowie at the last minute on February 20, 1974 and performed 'Seven Seas of Rhye').

MIDDLE LEFT: Former art and design student Freddie filled notebook after notebook with sketches, and designed Queen's logos himself. This is a reconstruction for the movie.

MIDDLE RIGHT: Filming at Heathrow Airport: one of Freddie's earliest jobs was as a baggage handler.

BOTTOM LEFT: Recreating the press conference for 1982's *Hot Space* album.

BOTTOM RIGHT: Even the small details on the crates had to be accurate.

OPPOSITE ABOVE: Gwilym Lee rocks a Brian May solo for the camera.

OPPOSITE BELOW: Cheap tricks to create vocal effects.

VOX

TOP: The full-size recreation of the Live Aid stage at Bovingdon Airfield.

MIDDLE: Drums, guitar and amps waiting for action on the set at Ridge Farm.

ABOVE: Taking a break from filming on the Ridge Farm set.

RIGHT: Is it a bird? Is it a plane? No, it's Mike Myers hurling obscenities from a window during filming in London.

ABOVE: The actors portraying Queen and Jim Beach, all dressed up for the video to 'I Want to Break Free'.

BELOW: Movie reconstruction of a leather bar: many in New York and Munich were frequented by Freddie.

OPPOSITE: Freddie / Rami at Live Aid, playing the first part of 'Bohemian Rhapsody'.

OVERLEAF: Queen rehearsing their Live Aid set in the movie; most other bands had less preparation.

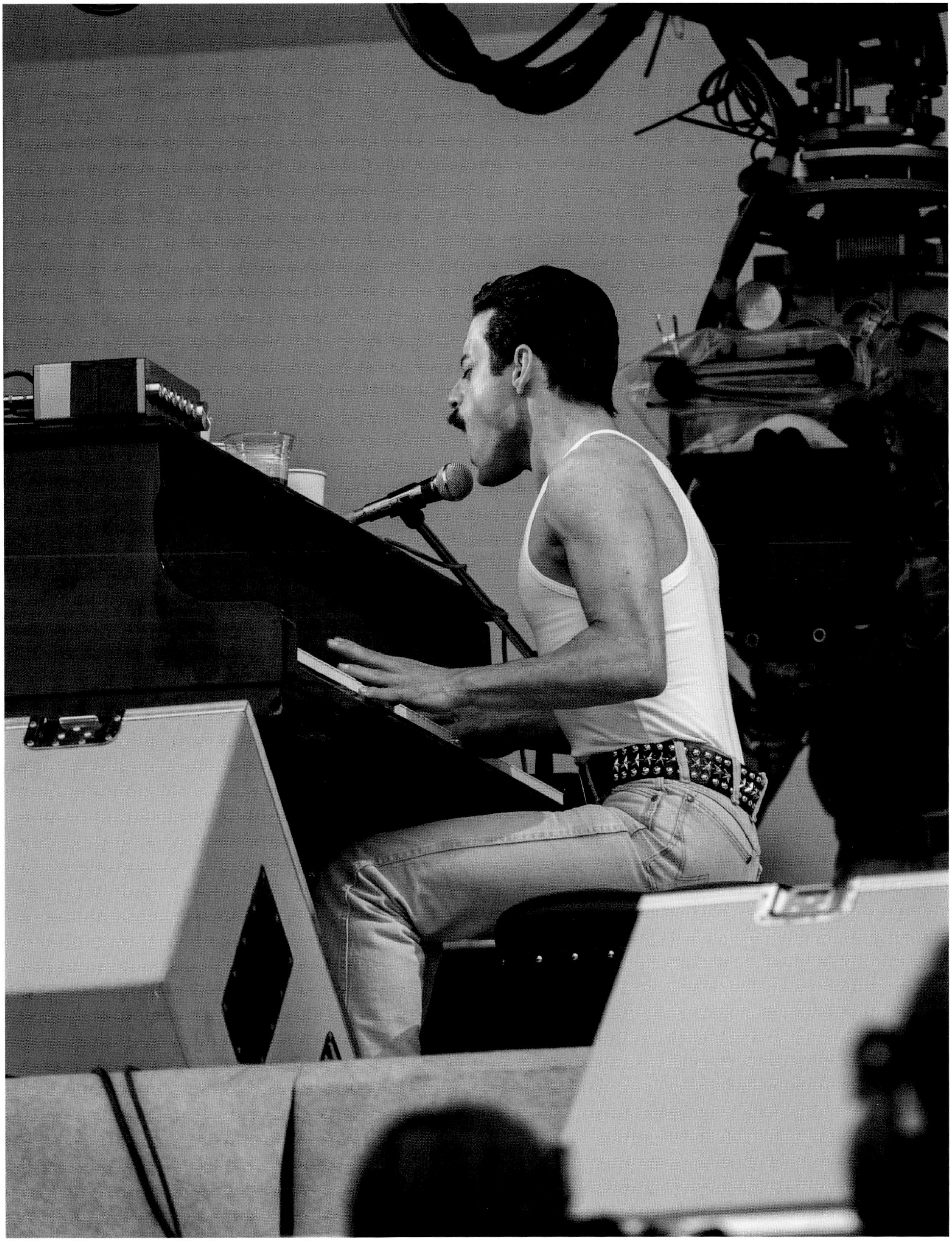

QUEEN

VOX
VOX
VOX
QUEEN

BOHEMIAN RHAPSODY

CHAPTER TWO

DON'T LOSE YOUR HEAD: FREDDIE MERCURY

FREDDIE MERCURY

FREDDIE MERCURY WAS BORN FARROKH BULSARA, ON SEPTEMBER 5, 1946, AND RAISED IN THE ZOROASTRIAN FAITH. HIS PARENTS BOMI AND JER WERE PARSIS FROM THE GUJARAT REGION OF MUMBAI, BUT HAD RELOCATED TO TANZANIA FOR BOMI'S JOB IN THE BRITISH COLONIAL OFFICE BY THE TIME FARROKH CAME ALONG. FARROKH'S YOUNGER SISTER KASHMIRA WAS BORN IN 1952.

Farrokh began piano lessons aged 8, and formed his first rock and roll band aged 12 at boarding school, where he also picked up the nickname Freddie. The family eventually relocated to the UK when he was 17 to escape the Zanzibar Revolution, but although the timing was exactly right for him to plug into the explosion of music and youth culture happening all around him, there were few signs that the awkward and somewhat shy Freddie of this period would metamorphose into the rock icon Freddie Mercury within just a few years.

He earned a diploma in art and graphic design from Isleworth Polytechnic in West London, enrolled at Ealing School of Art to study fashion design, and worked at Heathrow Airport and Kensington Market while moonlighting in a series of bands throughout the 1960s. But it was the arrival of Jimi Hendrix – performing 'Hey Joe' on the BBC pop show *Ready Steady Go!* in December 1966 – that really captivated Freddie's imagination. Entranced by his virtuoso performances and apparently effortless command of the stage, Freddie saw Hendrix in concert whenever possible: at least 14 times in a matter of months. "He had everything a rock star should have," Freddie said later. "He had all the style and presence. I would scour the country to see him whenever he played."

Another band Freddie saw a lot of was Smile, the pre-Queen project of Brian May and Roger Taylor. Freddie became part of their regular entourage, and when singer and bass player Tim Staffell quit, the band found itself in need of a new vocalist. A few bass players later, John Deacon joined, and by 1971 the quartet were performing as Queen. Freddie chose the name and designed the logo. Seizing on the word "Mercury" from the song "My Fairy King" on Queen's first album, he also changed his own name. Farrokh Bulsara was no more. Arise, Freddie Mercury.

If calling the band Queen seemed like an enthusiastic embracing of flamboyant camp, Freddie always batted those notions away, insisting instead that it just sounded appropriately "regal" for the world-conquering group they were determined to become. He would similarly sidestep all attention on his sexuality for the rest of his life and in public maintained the appearance of being in a long-term relationship with Mary Austin (not in itself untrue, but rather more complicated than the narrative the newspapers were fed). In the era of glam rock and its aftermath, where straight performers like David Bowie and Marc Bolan were experimenting with androgynous personas, his glamorous ostentation didn't seem particularly unusual.

Freddie and Queen, however, were anything but ordinary. What marked them out from the beginning was the way in which their music refused to be just one thing. Single albums would segue from hard rock to tender ballads, angry rants to crowd-pleasing anthems, prog rock fantasy epics to trad-jazz influenced knockabouts and seaside postcard humour. Freddie alone was responsible for examples of each. Every band member contributed songs (uniquely, all four members of Queen composed No.1 hit singles): the four very different individuals making up a whole that was eclectic but still somehow cohesive. Freddie said they were like four solo artists

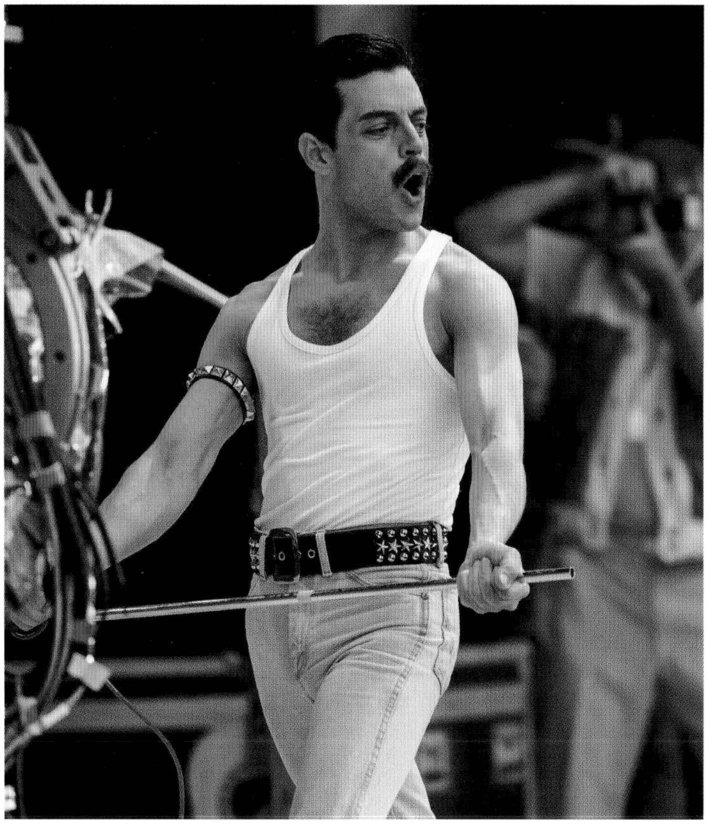

ABOVE: Rami rocks Freddie's famous half mic stand at Live Aid

contributing fulfillingly to a single project, making the idea of "going solo" redundant. As a unit, they sold – and continue to sell – tens of millions of records worldwide.

But Freddie did eventually embark on a solo side-career, releasing the album *Mr. Bad Guy* in 1985, after two years putting it together during rare moments of Queen down time. While never as successful alone as with the band, his 1987 single 'The Great Pretender' (a cover version of a 1950s hit by The Platters, the lyrics of which Freddie may well have strongly identified with) reached a respectable No.5 in the UK charts. Three years after Queen's barnstorming domination of Live Aid, he released a second solo album, *Barcelona*, in collaboration with the Italian opera singer Montserrat Caballé. That he was able to hold his own alongside the famous diva was testament to his vocal power and range, which stretched to at least three octaves.

His HIV diagnosis came in the early 80s, at a time when life expectancy with the illness was short. But while living under the shadow of AIDS curbed his energetic social and personal life, it never stopped him working. He finally succumbed on November 24, 1991. His will left the majority of his estate to Mary Austin, and a substantial amount to Jim Hutton, his partner for the last six years of his life.

The remaining Queen members founded the Mercury Phoenix Trust in 1992; a charity organization fighting and raising awareness of HIV and AIDS that remains active to this day. Posthumously, Freddie had another three top-ten solo hits, and some of his unfinished recordings were sensitively and painstakingly worked into Queen's final album, *Made in Heaven* in 1995. It sold more than 20 million copies: the band's fourth No.1 album in a row and seventh overall. The album cover features a photograph of the ten-foot statue of Freddie that stands in Montreux, Switzerland (where Queen recorded most of their output from 1978 onwards, and Mercury recorded his final vocals), overlooking Lake Geneva. The sleeve notes contain a dedication "to the immortal spirit of Freddie Mercury".

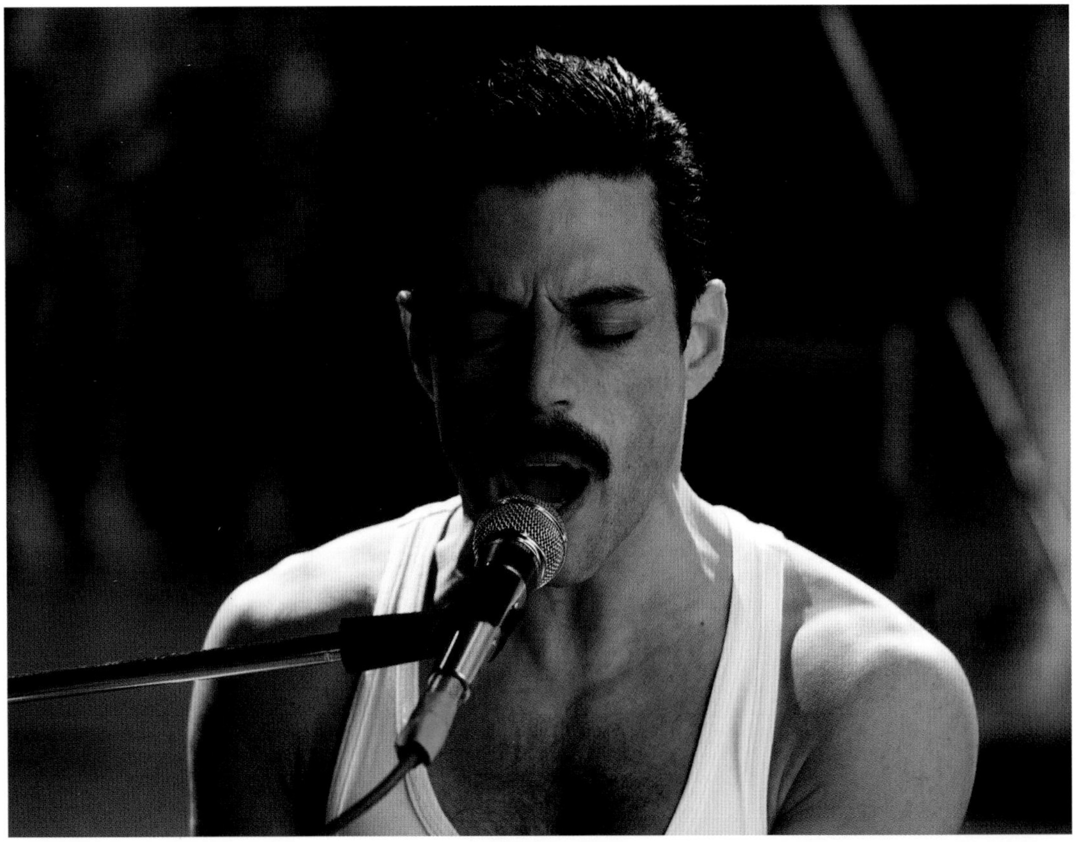

LEFT: "Mama… just killed a man…" Rami at the piano at Live Aid.

BELOW: Freddie's black leather look for the 1974 American tour recreated for the movie.

OPPOSITE ABOVE LEFT: Freddie / Rami in full leather club uniform in the Meatpacking District of New York.

OPPOSITE ABOVE RIGHT: Rami as Freddie. Yellow was one of Freddie's favourite colours. A variety of yellow rose is named after him.

OPPOSITE BELOW: Rami plays piano on the Ridge Farm set.

PREVIOUS PAGES LEFT and RIGHT: On stage in 1977 in the movie and in reality. Freddie's harlequin suit sold at auction in 2012 for £22,500.

ABOVE: The original white "angel" costume was designed by Zandra Rhodes and worn during Queen's first Japanese tour. **LEFT:** Rami in a carefully recreated costume.

BOHEMIAN
RHAPSODY

CHAPTER
THREE

WE ARE THE CHAMPIONS: THE CAST

UNDER PRESSURE

RAMI MALEK ON PLAYING FREDDIE MERCURY

RAMI SAID MALEK WAS BORN ON MAY 12, 1981: THE YEAR QUEEN TEAMED UP WITH DAVID BOWIE FOR THEIR NO.1 HIT 'UNDER PRESSURE'. HE WAS RAISED IN THE COPTIC ORTHODOX FAITH BY HIS EGYPTIAN PARENTS, WHO HAD RELOCATED TO LOS ANGELES BY THE TIME OF HIS BIRTH. HE ATTENDED HIGH SCHOOL IN SHERMAN OAKS, CALIFORNIA, BEFORE UNIVERSITY IN EVANSVILLE, INDIANA, FROM WHERE HE GRADUATED WITH A BACHELOR OF FINE ARTS DEGREE.

Rami's first professional acting role was an episode of *Gilmore Girls* in 2004, and he was a regular on the sitcom *The War at Home* between 2005 and 2007. He also appeared in the *Night at the Museum* and *Twilight* films; Paul Thomas Anderson's drama *The Master* (with Philip Seymour Hoffman); Spike Lee's *Oldboy* (with Josh Brolin); the car-chase movie *Need For Speed* (starring Aaron Paul and based on the popular videogame series); and Steven Spielberg's mini-series *The Pacific* (with his future *Bohemian Rhapsody* co-star Joseph Mazzello).

He achieved his biggest breakout success to date in 2015, scoring the lead role of Elliot in Universal's TV techno-thriller *Mr. Robot*. He was 34; Mercury's age when Queen released *The Game* and the *Flash Gordon* soundtrack. Two years later, Malek was on a replica Live Aid stage playing Freddie himself. Here, he discusses stepping into some of rock's most iconic shoes.

HOW DID YOU END UP WINNING THE ROLE OF FREDDIE MERCURY?

One of the first times I heard about this was [producer] Graham King phoning me and asking if I would come to Los Angeles. I was filming *Mr. Robot*, but I thought, 'I can't pass this up.' We had a six-hour meeting, and I could tell how passionate he was about the film. I think he knew that I appreciated Queen's music, and of course as an actor I was champing at the bit, even though I tried to restrain myself. I didn't want to come across as overly eager! But we just kept talking about Queen and Freddie throughout the evening until it got very late. Towards the end of the night I said, 'Well, I wish you the best of luck, whether it's me or you're thinking about other people for this too.' And he said, 'No, it's you.' It was a powerful moment because it's an immense responsibility, but one that I was very eager to take on. I remember going home with a stack of books and DVD documentaries, thinking, 'Wow…'

WHY DO YOU THINK QUEEN HAVE REMAINED POPULAR?

Songs like 'We Will Rock You' and 'We Are the Champions' epitomize what Queen did, I think. At their shows they brought everyone together. If people looked to their right or left, no matter what anybody's race or religion was, what they believed, or how they identified, everyone would be chanting the same song right back to that stage. That was what was electrifying and radical about Queen. They could get everyone to sing in unison, maybe in harmony at times.

OPPOSITE: Rami as Freddie relaxing in an ivory silk damask kimono. Freddie's love of Japanese art and culture began when Queen toured Japan in the mid 1970s.

WHAT DID YOU LEARN ABOUT FREDDIE WHILE WORKING ON THIS FILM?

His is very much an immigrant story. That was an insecurity for him, in terms of him feeling like he was searching for an identity and was someone who didn't quite fit in. Now, I think we can see that all of the things that made him so unique are what allowed him to persevere. But one of the themes of this film is very much identity. There are so many different faces of Freddie Mercury, and I don't think one is any truer than the other. He's also on this search for how he identifies sexually, and on this endless search for love. I think this film will allow his songs to resonate even more than they already did, by giving audiences that context of what he may have been going through or the questions he was trying to answer.

One thing about Freddie Mercury that's absolutely undeniable was his magnetism. Standing on stage brought something out of him that was like nothing else. In those moments he felt capable of anything, and I think what was magical about him was that exchange with everyone in the audience. He could just reach people almost as if they were the only person in the room no matter where they were: watching that stage from any row, hitting everyone all the way at the back of the theatre. That's what makes him one of the most unique and remarkable and revolutionary artists of our time – or any time.

HOW DID YOU DECIDE YOU WANTED TO PLAY HIM?

I tried to attack it the way I would any other role. If you strip away what he could do musically and on stage, there's a very complicated man at the center. So I figured if I could start there I would have the initial building blocks that give you the confidence to do all the other things like sing, and speak in his accent, and dominate a stage. I met [Movement Coach] Polly Bennett, and she talked to me about the impetus for why he moved the way he did and his heritage and things that would inform his mannerisms. It was about identifying all these little intricacies and then incorporating them into his physicality.

ABOVE and RIGHT: Rami studied the reasons behind Freddie's movement and mannerisms in order to perfect his performance.

DO THE WIGS AND THE MAKE-UP AND THE COSTUMES HELP YOU FIND THE CHARACTER, OR ARE THEY A DISTRACTION?

Well I had the most phenomenal make-up and hair designer, Jan Sewell. She made me the teeth; all kinds of versions of the teeth, because the first time we tried to get Freddie's exact size teeth and they were just massive! It just shows you what he was dealing with. She also did incredible work around my eyes, and just defining the structure of my face for different periods of his life. And we had a moustache – although he doesn't have that for the majority of the film. But it's all fulfilling, because it allows you that extra bit of confidence to know that you're getting that much closer to capturing his essence.

And then, getting to prance around a costume house, using that time to see how my moves were working in four-inch platforms or the tightest fitting satin pants, or an entire Lycra outfit… Every actor will tell you, it really just elevates your level of confidence and helps you solidify the character. And it was fun! When you dress as flamboyantly as Freddie did, it makes every day going into try on a costume feel like it's going to be a good time. I think most people identify Freddie as this short-haired, mustachioed, tank top wearing macho man. It was fairly astonishing to get to know the many other versions, and the very sweet side of him as well.

WHAT WAS IT LIKE HAVING TO REPLICATE QUEEN'S LIVE AID SET BEAT-FOR-BEAT FROM START TO FINISH?

I think Live Aid was a make-or-break moment for Freddie. He was coming off a solo album, and I think Live Aid was the moment where he re-captured that feeling of unity with his 'family' – the band. He was returning to the magic that only the four of them could create… in front of a massive crowd, not only at Wembley, but also via satellite to the world. I think it had the highest viewing figures of anything up to that date. The scope of it was not lost on me.

I'd never put my fingers on a piano before, so that was tricky and daunting. But it shows you that practically anything can be accomplished. There were moments when I didn't think it could possibly ever happen, and I thought that it was very questionable to start off the entire shoot with a sequence as major as Live Aid. But we pulled it off even though the whole idea seemed crazy. I think we proved ourselves wrong – or I proved myself wrong!

HOW IMPORTANT WAS THE INVOLVEMENT OF BRIAN MAY AND ROGER TAYLOR?

Having them involved was crucial. Their insight is obviously immense, and no one knows their story and this band more intimately than the two of them. To be able to talk to them on almost a daily basis was invaluable, and they were so kind and so classy about the whole thing. This film is a credit to them. It's very difficult to put your story in the hands of strangers, so it was lovely that we got to know them and feel closer to them and build this level of trust. We definitely did not want to let them down, and if there was ever anything that they thought wasn't working, it was always addressed. But having them cheer us on just added to our confidence levels. Knowing that they were there and watching and involved raised all of our games.

RIGHT: The actors playing the band members played the entire set from Live Aid in front of the cameras.

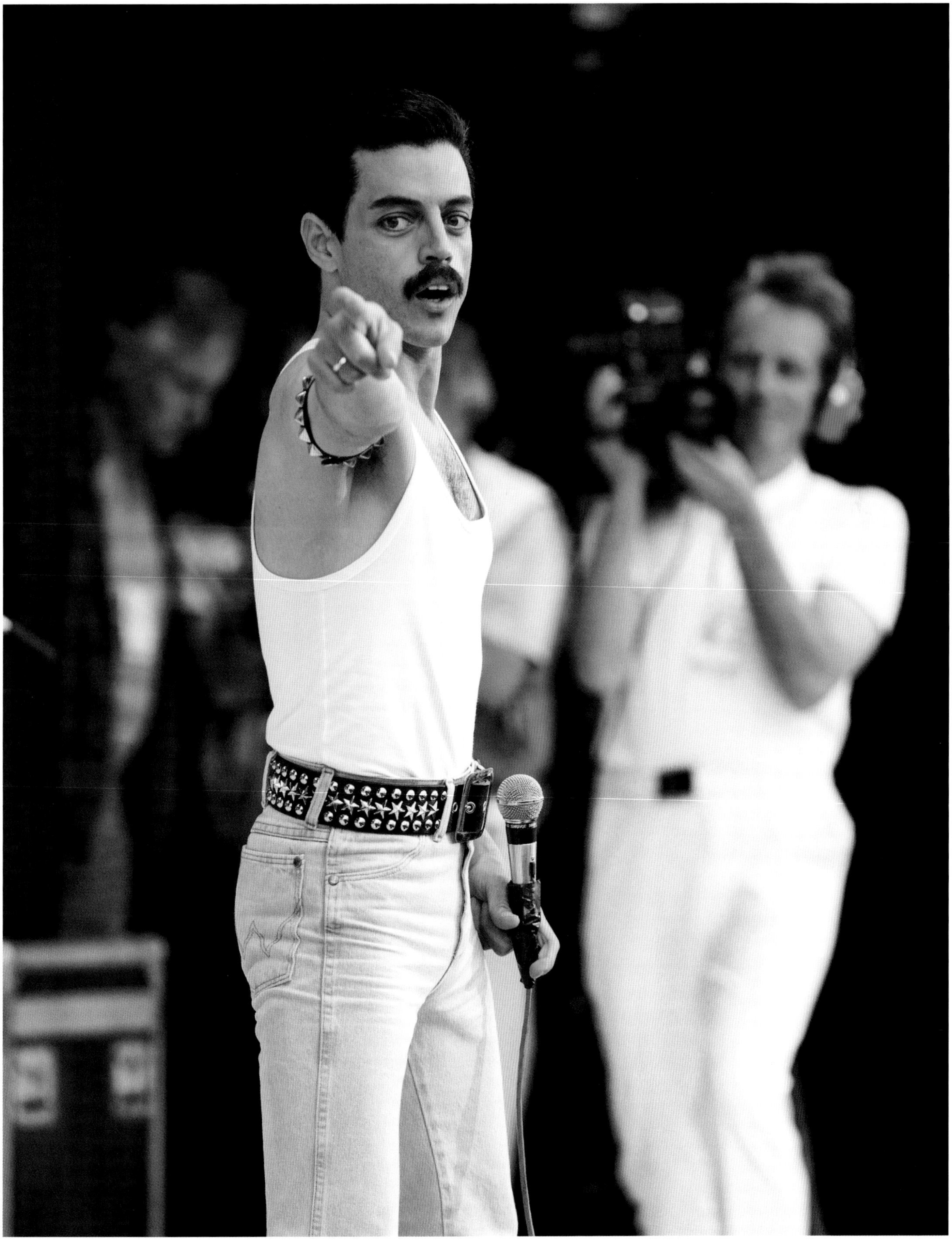

JOHN DEACON

JOHN DEACON WAS ACTUALLY QUEEN'S FOURTH BASS PLAYER, BUT HE WAS RECRUITED BEFORE THE RECORDING OF THEIR SELF-TITLED DEBUT ALBUM IN 1973. A MUTUAL FRIEND INTRODUCED HIM TO BRIAN MAY AND ROGER TAYLOR AT A DISCO IN 1971. A REGULAR ON THE LONDON GIG SCENE AT THE TIME, HE'D PLAYED IN HIS FIRST BAND AT THE AGE OF 14, AND THE FACT THAT HE WAS STUDYING ELECTRONICS AT CHELSEA COLLEGE MADE HIM HANDY WITH AMPLIFIERS AND OTHER STAGE EQUIPMENT, IN ADDITION TO HIS TALENT ON THE BASS AND NATURAL RHYTHM.

John's most immediate predecessor in Queen, Doug Bogie, had been dismissed for being too showy, but the quiet Deacon was an immediate fit: the final piece of the Queen puzzle; a line-up that would remain unchanged until Freddie Mercury's death two decades later. Never a fan of the limelight, he was rarely interviewed compared to his band mates.

His first solo writing credit was 'Misfire', on Queen's third album, 1974's *Sheer Heart Attack*; his songwriting was subsequently behind 'You're My Best Friend', 'Spread Your Wings', 'I Want to Break Free', and the colossal worldwide hit 'Another One Bites the Dust'. A fan of soul music, funk and Motown as well as rock, much of the impetus driving Queen's controversial disco detour *Hot Space* in 1982 was his. The change in direction led to some acrimony within the band, although their differences had been thrashed out by the time of the next album, 1984's *The Works*.

Following Mercury's death in 1991 and the *Made in Heaven* album in 1995, he only played with May and Taylor three more times before retiring in 1997.

JOSEPH MAZZELLO

Joseph Mazzello was the child star of Steven Spielberg's *Jurassic Park* in 1993, aged just nine. After studying at the University of Southern California, he made his acting comeback as an adult in 2010 with roles in the TV mini-series *The Pacific* (produced by Spielberg and Tom Hanks and also featuring Rami Malek in the cast) and David Fincher's film *The Social Network*.

He views John Deacon as an "accidental rock star" who played the role of a sort of "younger brother" to Freddie Mercury. "He was the youngest member of Queen and the last to join," Mazzello explains, "and whereas I think the other guys grew up wanting to be famous musicians or rock stars, John was perfectly content working with electronics and just playing music for fun. Queen just sort of happened to him and snowballed, and before he knew it they were touring America and Japan. I think it took him a while to find himself, but he was an integral part of the band, despite being more introverted than the rest of them."

Like his movie band mates, Mazzello worked hard to be seen to be playing his bass for real on screen, learning all the necessary songs over an intense six-week preparation period. "The first time we heard ourselves play together was a really exciting moment," he recalls. "I just felt like, right, I'm actually doing this!"

OPPOSITE: Joseph Mazzello as Queen's bass player John Deacon, on stage at Live Aid.

QUEEN
Fender
Fender PRECISION BASS

ABOVE: "I can't tell you how many bass players have asked me if I'm playing for real…" (Joseph Mazzello)

BELOW: Mazzello's Live Aid wig was dubbed "The Mushroom". The wig received its own round of applause at the end of filming.

OPPOSITE: John Deacon playing live.

Fender
Fender

BRIAN MAY

Brian May formed his first band whilst still a schoolboy in the Greater London area, playing a guitar he'd built himself. Whilst studying Mathematics and Physics at Imperial College, London, in the late 1960s, he formed the band Smile with drummer Roger Taylor and bassist/ vocalist Tim Staffell: the group that would eventually evolve into Queen when Staffell quit and Freddie Mercury joined.

A virtuoso with unique idiosyncracies (he continues to play his self-built "Red Special" and uses coins instead of plectrums), he cites Hank Marvin, the Beatles, The Who, Jimi Hendrix, Led Zeppelin, Jeff Beck, Eric Clapton and Rory Gallagher among his primary influences, as well as "trad-jazz" acts like the Temperance Seven. Some of his most significant compositions for Queen were 'We Will Rock You', 'Hammer To Fall', 'Fat Bottomed Girls' and 'I Want It All'.

Continuing to enjoy a successful career both with modern iterations of Queen and solo, he is frequently voted one of the greatest rock guitarists of all time. But his achievements extend beyond music. He maintained his interest in astrophysics throughout the Queen years and beyond, finally achieving a doctorate (for his thesis *A Survey of Radial Velocities in the Zodiacal Dust Cloud*) from Imperial College in 2007 – 33 years after dropping out in favour of the band. He also remains a committed environmental and animal rights activist, forming the organization Save Me in 2010 to campaign against fox hunting, badger culling and other issues. He was awarded the CBE in 2006.

GWILYM LEE

Gwilym Lee was born in 1983 and was acting at the Royal Shakespeare Company by the age of 16. Early television roles included episodes of *Lewis* and *Doctors*, and more significant parts in *Land Girls*, *Midsomer Murders* and *Jamestown*. On film he had roles in *The Tourist* (2010, with Johnny Depp and Angelina Jolie), and *The Last Witness* (2018, with Alex Pettyfer) among others.

He plays guitar to the extent that there's been no need to use a stand-in for him in fretboard close-ups ("I take a bit of pride in that!"), but says the intimidating job of pretending to play Brian May's guitar lines in front of their composer was made easier by May's easygoing demeanour.

"He's just a warmhearted individual," Lee grins. "I felt kind of safe in his presence. He recognizes that I'm not a musician at his level, and he recognizes my job is not to try and match him musically, but to bring across his character. The day we filmed the scene of me playing the 'Bohemian Rhapsody' solo, he appeared halfway through when nobody had known he was going to turn up that day. At the end the crew were all sympathising with me that it must have been terrifying. But it actually wasn't, because he's so supportive. He told me he usually grimaces at one point in that solo because there's a bend in a note that's a really big stretch. Stuff like that is really useful."

LEFT and BELOW: Gwilym Lee as Brian May, on stage and behind the scenes at Live Aid.
ABOVE: Brian May at Live Aid, 1985.

"BRIAN MAY IS JUST A WARMHEARTED INDIVIDUAL!" Gwilym Lee

OPPOSITE: Gwilym Lee sports the Bohemian look on the Ridge Farm set.

ABOVE: The Two Brians. Gwilym Lee with the real deal on the Ridge Farm set.

LEFT: Gwilym in '*Coronation Street*' drag for the 'I Want To Break Free' music video.

INSET: A copy of Brian's famous "Red Special" guitar, built for the movie.

ROGER TAYLOR

ROGER TAYLOR, LIKE HIS LIFELONG FRIEND BRIAN MAY, WAS A FOUNDER MEMBER OF THE BAND SMILE. HE GREW UP IN CORNWALL, BUT MOVED TO LONDON IN THE LATE 1960S TO STUDY DENTISTRY AT THE LONDON HOSPITAL MEDICAL COLLEGE, LATER SWITCHING TO A BIOLOGY COURSE AT EAST LONDON POLYTECHNIC.

Taylor met May in 1968 when he responded to May's ad in search of a drummer. And for a time starting in 1969 he ran a stall on Kensington Market with Freddie Mercury.

He formed his first band at primary school (playing the ukulele), and his next as a teenager, by which point he had taken up and then abandoned the guitar in favour of the drums. He was inspired by The Who's Keith Moon, Led Zeppelin's John Bonham, and Mitch Mitchell of the Jimi Hendrix Experience, as well as the legendary jazz drummer Buddy Rich. May has said that just the sound of Taylor tuning up is better than that of most drummers playing normally.

'Radio Ga Ga', 'These Are the Days of Our Lives', 'A Kind of Magic' and 'I'm In Love With My Car' are among his compositional credits for Queen. He's also had a successful career away from the band: as a solo artist; with his other project The Cross (in which he sang and played rhythm guitar); as a guest musician on albums by the likes of Elton John, Gary Numan and Roger Daltrey; and as a producer.

BEN HARDY

Ben Hardy was born in 1991 and made his professional acting debut on stage at the age of 21 in a successful London run of David Hare's *The Judas Kiss*. He went on to play Peter Beale for two years on the BBC soap *Eastenders*, and the male lead in the BBC adaptation of Wilkie Collins' *The Woman in White*. On film he's had roles in *X-Men: Apocalypse, Mary Shelley* and *Only the Brave.*

He says that one of the aspects of Roger Taylor that he latched onto for his portrayal was the theatricality of Taylor's drumming. "He has a few 'showman' things that he does," he explains, "like spinning his drumsticks, and this whipping motion on the snare drum. I tried to use all of that. He also has a particular drumming face. They say every drummer has one, and no one knows quite why they do it – even themselves. It's just very natural to them to make a certain face when they're drumming, and it's often quite hilarious if you study them!"

Ben says he was nervous to meet the real Roger, having been researching him by watching enough video footage to "feel like a stalker". An impromptu drum lesson where Taylor challenged Hardy to "sit down and show me what you can do," was also somewhat terrifying. "But he was very helpful and he taught me a lot," Hardy reflects. "We're physically and vocally quite different, but my job is not to impersonate him. It's to give the strongest essence of him I can while serving the purpose of this film."

OPPOSITE: Ben Hardy as Queen's drummer Roger Taylor, banging away at Live Aid.

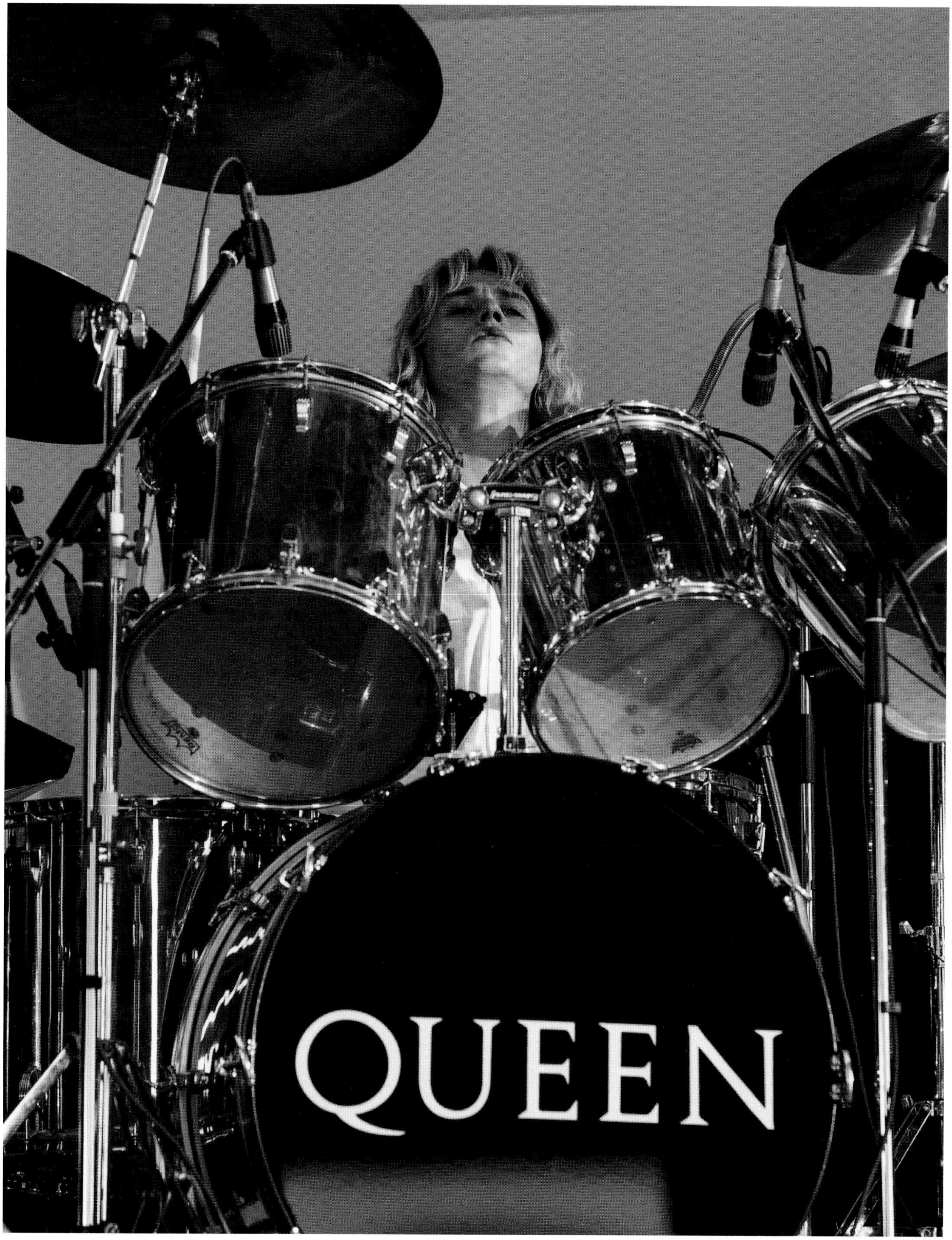
QUEEN

"ROGER HAS A FEW 'SHOWMAN' THINGS THAT HE DOES..." Ben Hardy

ABOVE: It's not just about drumming: Hardy had to learn to spin the sticks too.

RIGHT: Roger Taylor – the real deal.

BELOW: Every drummer has his "drumming face"; this is Ben Hardy's.

OPPOSITE: Down on the Ridge Farm set during filming.

MARY AUSTIN

MARY AUSTIN BEGAN DATING FREDDIE MERCURY IN SEPTEMBER OF 1970, AND WITHIN FIVE MONTHS THE COUPLE WERE LIVING TOGETHER (WITH TWO CATS) IN KENSINGTON; FIRST IN A BEDSIT AND LATER IN A FLAT. IT WAS, FROM THE BEGINNING, A DEEP AND INTENSE RELATIONSHIP, AND ONE THAT WOULD CONTINUE FOR THE REST OF THEIR LIVES.

The romance may have ended as Freddie and Mary both came to terms with his sexuality, but their intense connection was never broken. When they met, Mary was working at the fashionable Biba; nowadays a mainstay of department stores, but then a single boutique on Kensington High Street, boasting the cutting edge of fashion. The top musicians and models of the day regularly visited the shop: as much for the beauty of its staff as of its merchandise. Mercury became a regular visitor. "Occasionally he was brave enough to come in on his own," Austin remembered, "but most of the time he'd come along with Roger [Taylor] or somebody and smile and say hello in passing… which became quite often."[1]

The initial phase of their relationship ended when Freddie could no longer keep his affairs with men secret from Mary. "He said, 'I think I'm bisexual,'" she recalled. "I said, 'I think you're gay.'"[2] But while the truth physically separated them, their mutual acceptance of it brought them spiritually closer together. Mary moved out, but only to a neighbouring apartment, and the pair remained close until Freddie's death. He bequeathed her half of his considerable estate, including Garden Lodge mansion, in his will.

"People always ask me about my sexuality," Mercury once said, "but I couldn't fall in love with a man the same way as I have with Mary."[3] She has generally been assumed to be the subject of the Mercury-penned Queen song 'Love of My Life'.

LUCY BOYNTON

Lucy Boynton was born in 1994, and made her screen debut at the age of just 12, playing the young Beatrix Potter in *Miss Potter*. Since then she's appeared regularly on television (*Sense & Sensibility, Gypsy*) and on film (*Sing Street, I Am the Pretty Thing That Lives in the House, Murder on the Orient Express).*

She says that her portrayal of Mary Austin in *Bohemian Rhapsody* is very much a fictionalized version. "Mary is an incredibly private person," she explains, "so we've tried to make this 'Mary' separate from the real Mary Austin to kind of protect her."

The essence of the character, however, remains the aspect that immediately impressed Lucy when she first read the screenplay: her indelible bond with Freddie Mercury. The scene in which she accepts a ring from Freddie is, she says, a particular stand-out for her, proving that their relationship "goes much deeper than just a romance or a piece of paper that says you're married. It's a joining of two souls, and I think that's really beautiful and sad and difficult. They recognize this thing that is so deep and intrinsic. Rather than just, 'be my wife,' the ring represents, 'Be my ally; be my partner in this world and in this life'. Their relationship is so important to both of their existences that it carries on even after they realize they can't be together as a couple."

[1] *Freddie Mercury: The Untold Story* (Documentary, directors Rudi Dolezal & Hannes Rossacher), 2000

[2] Mary Austin interview with David Wigg, *Daily Express*, 2000

[3] *Freddie Mercury: His Life in His Own Words*, Greg Brooks & Simon Lupton (Omnibus Press, 2009)

OPPOSITE: Lucy Boynton as Mary Austin, Freddie Mercury's first love.

TOP: The actors playing Mary and Freddie at home in their Kensington flat.

ABOVE: The set for Mary and Freddie's bedroom.

ABOVE RIGHT: Lucy backstage on the Live Aid set.

RIGHT: Helping Freddie choose a Biba outfit.

OPPOSITE ABOVE: Mary Austin and Freddie Mercury.

OPPOSITE: Lucy backstage at Live Aid with Rami in the movie.

"IT'S A JOINING OF TWO SOULS..." Lucy Boynton

JIM BEACH

JIM BEACH ENTERED QUEEN'S STORY IN 1975 AS THEIR LAWYER, JUST AS THE BAND WERE REACHING THE PEAK OF THEIR EARLIEST SUCCESS. 'KILLER QUEEN' HAD BECOME THEIR BREAKTHROUGH HIT, DRIVING SALES OF THE *SHEER HEART ATTACK* LP INTO THE HUNDREDS OF THOUSANDS OF COPIES IN THE UK AND AMERICA, AND SIGNIFICANTLY BOOSTING SALES OF THE PREVIOUS TWO ALBUMS.

But the band were still only earning £60 a week from their then record label, Trident. Beach, who at that time was a music partner at London law firm Harbottle & Lewis, was the man who extricated them from that contract: a process that took months but yielded substantial rewards. In 1978 he dismantled another contract between the band and their then manager John Reid, and from that point on became a permanent part of Queen's management structure, giving up his law partnership to do so.

While often described as such, he was never technically Queen's manager, since, after Reid, the band carefully built a new system whereby they were managing themselves. But with Beach handling all of Queen's legal and contractual business, and overseeing their various companies and assets, along with their solo side projects, it's a moot point. Away from Queen he has also managed Chris Rea and others, produced feature films and television specials, and undertaken theatre projects with Monty Python and Stephen Sondheim. And he was, of course, one of the driving forces behind the behemoth success of Queen's stage musical *We Will Rock You*. He is a Trustee of the EMI Music Sound Foundation, the Mercury Phoenix Trust and START.

TOM HOLLANDER

Tom Hollander is a prolific British film, television and stage actor. He began his career with an award-winning performance in a 1992 production of William Congreve's *The Way of the World* at the Lyric Hammersmith Theatre, and went on to success in the likes of the *Pirates of the Caribbean* films and *In the Loop*, and as the title character of the BBC sit-com *Rev*. In 2017 he won BAFTA's Best Supporting Actor award for playing Corky in the BBC's acclaimed John Le Carre adaptation *The Night Manager*.

"My older sister got [1975 album] *A Night At The Opera*," he says of his introduction to Queen's music, "and I remember playing it a lot. This was in the mid-80s, when Queen were not cool and you were supposed to be into new wave bands like the Cure, who I actually didn't really have any taste for. But Queen were so brilliant. Their musicianship and versatility were amazing."

Tom was able to meet Jim Beach to prepare for his role in *Bohemian Rhapsody*, and found him "a very interesting man. He's a rather old fashioned sort of Englishman, but dressed in the clothing of someone in the rock and roll industry. He's very watchful, and clearly extremely intelligent and a brilliant strategist for Queen. And he continues to be."

OPPOSITE: Tom Hollander as Queen's lawyer and "manager" Jim Beach.

"HE'S AN OLD FASHIONED ENGLISHMAN IN ROCK AND ROLL CLOTHING."

Tom Hollander

OPPOSITE: Crunching the numbers and signing the deals: Tom Hollander as Jim Beach.

ABOVE: Hollander as Jim Beach (left). He negotiated the end of John Reid's (Aidan Gillen, right) contract to manage Queen.

TOP: Roger Taylor (centre) and Jim Beach (right) taking a train between concerts, 1982.

JOHN REID

In 1975, Queen were in the process of separating from their then representatives at Trident Studios, and were therefore in need of a new manager. Enter John Reid, a Scottish impresario, already working with Elton John but in the market for a band.

With perfect timing, EMI executive David Croker called him to ask if Queen might be of interest. Reid was keen to see if they could play live (since this would be essential if they were to crack America), so an impromptu gig was arranged at Ridge Farm. Reid believes that several other potential managers (including Led Zeppelin's Peter Grant) had been invited, but that he was the only one who showed up and so got the job by default.

Whether or not that's true, his relationship with the band lasted for the two years that encompassed their stratospheric rise to stardom. It began well, with Reid an early champion of 'Bohemian Rhapsody', but by 1977 the band were increasingly taking charge of their own affairs, and of the opinion that Reid was unable to devote sufficient time to Queen while also managing Elton. Jim Beach was brought in to negotiate the liquidation of a contract that still had a number of years to run, but the process was amicable. He remained on friendly terms with the band, and particularly Freddie Mercury.

AIDAN GILLEN

Irish actor Aidan Gillen got one of his earliest breaks on British television in the 1999 Channel 4 drama *Queer As Folk*. On stage he won a Tony award for his work in the 2004 Broadway revival of Harold Pinter's *The Caretaker*, which in turn led to his casting in HBO's acclaimed series *The Wire*. His previous film work has included blockbusters like *The Dark Knight Rises* and smaller projects like *Calvary*, while on TV he's had further standout roles in *Game of Thrones* and *Peaky Blinders*.

In *Bohemian Rhapsody* he's introduced as John Reid in the scene recreating the showcase Ridge Farm gig: the camera initially focusing solely on his clapping hands. "You think they're playing to a full auditorium," Gillen explains, "but then you realize that it's just John Reid and Paul Prenter sitting out there in the darkness."

This is artistic license: in reality Prenter wasn't there. But Reid did employ Prenter, and was responsible for introducing him to Mercury. "Reid was a very clever guy," Gillen believes, "but according to our script at least, he was uncharacteristically duped by Prenter, who was an opportunist who wanted to become Freddie's personal manager."

Gillen didn't get to meet the real Reid, but says the costumes and sets can't help but add to his own authenticity. "The first scenes I worked on were in the EMI offices," he remembers, "and it really was like stepping back into the 1970s. Things like that give you confidence. I've got some great shoes, and an open-necked shirt. And I'll be wearing a grey crushed velvet suit later, I believe…"

OPPOSITE TOP: Aidan Gillen as Queen's early manager John Reid. **OPPOSITE BELOW:** John Reid with Freddie Mercury in 1977.

PAUL PRENTER

PAUL PRENTER FIRST ENTERED QUEEN'S STORY IN 1977. A FORMER BOYFRIEND OF THEIR THEN-MANAGER JOHN REID, HE HAD ESCAPED THE TROUBLES IN BELFAST BY MAKING THE MOVE TO LONDON, WHERE REID HAD GIVEN HIM EMPLOYMENT AS A RUNNER. HE BECAME PART OF THE BAND'S ORBIT IN THAT CAPACITY, BUT WAS SOON A KEY PART OF FREDDIE MERCURY'S PERSONAL ENTOURAGE, AND A CLOSE FRIEND OF THE SINGER.

By 1982 Prenter was officially Mercury's Personal Assistant, annoying the rest of Queen with his unwanted opinions and apparent ability to influence Mercury's professional decisions. Less professionally, he was also a facilitator of Mercury's drug use and energetic sex life, particularly around the era's gay scenes in Munich and New York. His persistent whispering to Mercury that he was bigger than the rest of Queen and would be better off as a solo artist understandably caused considerable friction within the band. He also, having self-appointed himself Mercury's personal manager, refused most interviews on his so-called client's behalf, alienating Mercury from the media, particularly in the United States.

Events came to a head in 1986 when Prenter took a step too far. Mercury, having himself moved into Garden Lodge, had given Prenter the keys to his flat on Stafford Terrace: letting him stay there as a favour. Prenter threw a chaotic impromptu party and trashed the apartment. Mercury finally cut Prenter out of his life, but Prenter exacted his revenge a few months later, selling details of Mercury's sex life and AIDS diagnosis for £32,000 to tabloid newspaper *The Sun*. Mercury was devastated by the betrayal.

ALLEN LEECH

Dublin-born actor Allen Leech discovered his love of the stage in a school production of *The Wizard of Oz*, aged 11. He graduated from Trinity College, Dublin, with a Masters degree in Drama and Theatre Studies, and went onto continued regular theatre work; roles in the hit ITV series *Downton Abbey*, the BBC's *The Tudors*, and HBO's *Rome*; and appearances in films such as *The Sweeney*, *The Imitation Game* and *The Hunter's Prayer*.

The understanding he arrived at when preparing to play Paul Prenter was that Prenter was "quite a malevolent force within Freddie Mercury's life. Freddie liked to take care of people, be it financially or emotionally, and always felt guilty if he let people down. So anyone who had the ability to then play on that – and I think Paul Prenter definitely did – could use it to their advantage. Paul sold the story to *The Sun* that Freddie had AIDS and had a string of lovers. We see the start of their relationship as friends and confidantes, and then the realization that Paul was only ever there for himself."

Leech is sensitive, however, to the fact that he's playing a person who existed in real life, with all the complexity that entails. "He can't just be a two-dimensional villain," he reflects. "There is a certain amount of respect you have to give to the person, as well as to his role in the story and how it's being told. You always have to find that balance."

OPPOSITE: Allen Leech as Freddie Mercury's "personal manager" / hanger-on Paul Prenter.

"HE CAN'T JUST BE A TWO-DIMENSIONAL VILLAIN."

Allen Leech

ABOVE: The actors playing Paul Prenter and Freddie Mercury on a post-nightclub/early morning foray into New York's Meatpacking District.

LEFT: An intimate moment in the studio for Mercury and Prenter from the movie.

OPPOSITE: Prenter eventually sold Mercury's secrets to a British tabloid newspaper. Here Allen Leech reads on set.

RIO IS BRAZIL'S MOST
FOUND
Police Officer Killed
Rio's Morro da

RAY FOSTER
MIKE MYERS

MIKE MYERS INTRODUCED 'BOHEMIAN RHAPSODY' TO A NEW GENERATION IN THE CLASSIC 1991 COMEDY *WAYNE'S WORLD*. IN THE *BOHEMIAN RHAPSODY* MOVIE HE PLAYS EMI EXECUTIVE RAY FOSTER, WHO IS RELUCTANT TO RELEASE THE SIX-MINUTE EPIC AS A SINGLE. "NO ONE," HE SAYS, "WILL EVER BANG THEIR HEADS TO THIS..."

Here, the film's band members recall filming this memorable scene:

"It was surreal. For me, part of growing up was watching the *Austin Powers* movies, and for other people it would be *Wayne's World*."

Ben Hardy (Roger Taylor)

"Growing up when I did in the US, there was *Saturday Night Live*, *Wayne's World*, *Austin Powers*, *So I Married An Axe Murderer*... This guy is someone that I think I quoted more than anyone else in the world. I think more things came out of my mouth that he originally said than I originally said."

Joseph Mazzello (John Deacon)

"Everybody knows the scene in the car in *Wayne's World* when they're listening to 'Bohemian Rhapsody'. So to have him in this film was like this beautiful moment of synergy."

Gwilym Lee (Brian May)

"He came on set and he was the character. He took it very seriously. It wasn't like he came in to like have a laugh. He came in as professional as anyone else there, wanting to make sure he gave this role, as compact as it was in the movie, every single thing he had."

Joseph Mazzello

"He came on set fully made up and in costume, and fully in character, and he'd got it worked out to a tee. He kind of plays it as this slightly gruff, old-school music manager, with the medallions and the chest wig, the aviator glasses, the kind of curly hair, slightly fake tan."

Gwilym Lee

"He took it very seriously. He stayed in his Yorkshire accent, his British accent, the entire time, on and off set. He's the kind of guy who just can't not be funny. He was just cracking us up all day long, and it felt like he wasn't even trying to."

Ben Hardy

OPPOSITE ABOVE: "Nobody will ever bang their head to 'Bohemian Rhapsody' – Mike Myers as EMI executive Ray Foster.

OPPOSITE BELOW: "He's the kind of guy who just can't not be funny" – Ben Hardy on Mike Myers.

BOHEMIAN
RHAPSODY

CHAPTER
FOUR

LET ME ENTERTAIN YOU: COSTUMES, HAIR & MAKE-UP

TRANSFORMING RAMI
FREDDIE'S FEATURES

Rami Malek's performance as Freddie Mercury takes the iconic singer from 1970 through to 1985. With Mercury undergoing multiple changes of style and image over that 15 years, it was the job of Hair and Make-Up designer Jan Sewell and her department to believably transform the actor without turning him into a caricature. "Freddie was an incredible young man," she believes. "The visual journey of his life was what was so appealing about this project." Here, she details the process of turning Rami into Freddie.

FACE

"Often the camera will make things look more than they are, so we tested and tested lots of teeth to see how much they changed Rami's face. Freddie was very aware of his teeth. He never did get them fixed, and I'm sure he could have afforded to. He chose not to, and a lot of what he did was hiding them: there were lots of mouth movements. It was really important that we got the right size that Rami felt he could act with them and be able to mimic those mannerisms. In fact he had teeth made way before I met him, which he was using to get used to them. He'd done a lot of work beforehand."

HAIR

"Then, of course it's the multitude of wigs. Rami's got fabulous hair and we most definitely could have used it except he was coming off of his show, *Mr. Robot*, where he had the tightest haircut. So, in fact, Rami wears a wig all the way through *Bohemian Rhapsody*, in every scene: even for the really short hair Freddie had at Live Aid, because we just couldn't get Rami's hair to grow in time.

"The first time we see him, in 1970, Freddie's hair was naturally curly. If you brush out curly hair and it gets long it's got quite a wave to it. So we started off with a shorter look, trying to make him look as young as possible. We've got lovely scenes of his meeting Mary in Biba. Then when his career starts to take off and he becomes a rock star, we go into a shorter fringe, where he's growing his hair out, and wearing makeup on stage.

"Then later on his hair got slightly shorter again, until we go into what we call, 'the long-short', which is when he started to cut his hair, and the first time we see him with his moustache."

MOUSTACHE

"We also tried tons of moustaches. We had to get those right. With the longer hair he had to have a slightly fuller moustache, and then when we see him at Live Aid everything's much, much smaller. Rami's got the tightest little wig on and a slightly smaller moustache to match."

LEFT: Rami as the awkward younger Freddie in Biba.

ABOVE: Freddie at work on the set of Ridge Farm.

BELOW: Rami's 1980s Freddie in front of a gold disc for Queen's *Greatest Hits Vol 1*. That compilation is still the UK's biggest selling album of all time.

OPPOSITE ABOVE: Rami as Freddie in red leather recreating the Madison Square Garden, New York concert.

OPPOSITE BELOW: Scene 160A, take 8, and... action!

BOHEMIAN
RHAPSODY
SLATE
160A
TAKE
8
CAM:
NEWTON THOMAS SIGEL ASC
A006

COSTUMES
BECOMING QUEEN

FREDDIE MERCURY CARED ABOUT WHAT HE WORE. *BOHEMIAN RHAPSODY'S* COSTUME DESIGNER JULIAN DAY MADE IT HIS MISSION TO FULLY RESPECT THAT.

"Freddie was very conscious of what he was saying about himself through his clothes," Day says. "And even though he was quite flamboyant, he was quite macho as well. That duality was very interesting. I've done a couple of other biopic films where people have asked me to do slight changes to the costumes, but for this one I definitely wanted to stay as accurate as possible."

Bohemian Rhapsody was an enormous undertaking for Day's department, who were responsible for kitting out hundreds of extras as well as making sure no outfit appears twice in the film. The number of costumes used ran to thousands, with the four members of Queen alone needing an entire bus to house their wardrobe.

For Freddie personally, Day planned the wardrobe choices according to beats that the narrative needed to hit. For his early days working on Kensington market, he wanted Freddie dressed in the sort of vintage 1930s gear he would have been selling. Later, there's more colour and ostentation, like the harlequin outfit Freddie wore at several high profile concerts in the 1970s (the genuine article of which sold at auction in London in 2012 for £22,500). And of course, there was the crown-and-cape ensemble, and the infamous "angel", which Freddie wore at the Budokan, Tokyo, during their first Japanese tour in May, 1975.

For the latter, original designer Zandra Rhodes provided assistance. "Zandra made quite a lot of their stage wear," says Day, "and we went to her studio and she reproduced a few things for us. Apparently the story of the white winged outfit Freddie wore at Budokan is that Freddie went to Zandra because she was making things for him, and he saw a wedding dress and said, 'I really love that, but obviously I can't wear the full thing.' So, she chopped it in half and gave it to him. I don't know whether it's true or not but it's a great story!"

For Freddie's leather look of the late 70s and 80s, Day referenced the iconic homoerotic photographs of Robert Mapplethorpe, and William Friedkin's 1980 crime film *Cruising* (starring Al Pacino as an undercover cop hunting a serial killer who targets the gay club scene).

And while you might think that Freddie's Live Aid costume would be the simplest of all to recreate, even that apparently plain white vest became the subject of careful attention. "Rami was great on every detail," says Day of his star. "We made a vest for him – or rather about fifteen vests for him – and then he came in a couple of days before shooting and just said, 'You know, I was looking at pictures of Freddie again and I'm just wondering if we can just scoop a little bit more out of the vest at the front.' We looked at pictures together and he was absolutely right. Time was quite short, but we went back and quickly altered all these vests. We only scooped another half an inch out, but that half an inch makes a big difference."

OPPOSITE: A glimpse beneath the recreated Zandra Rhodes "angel" costume.

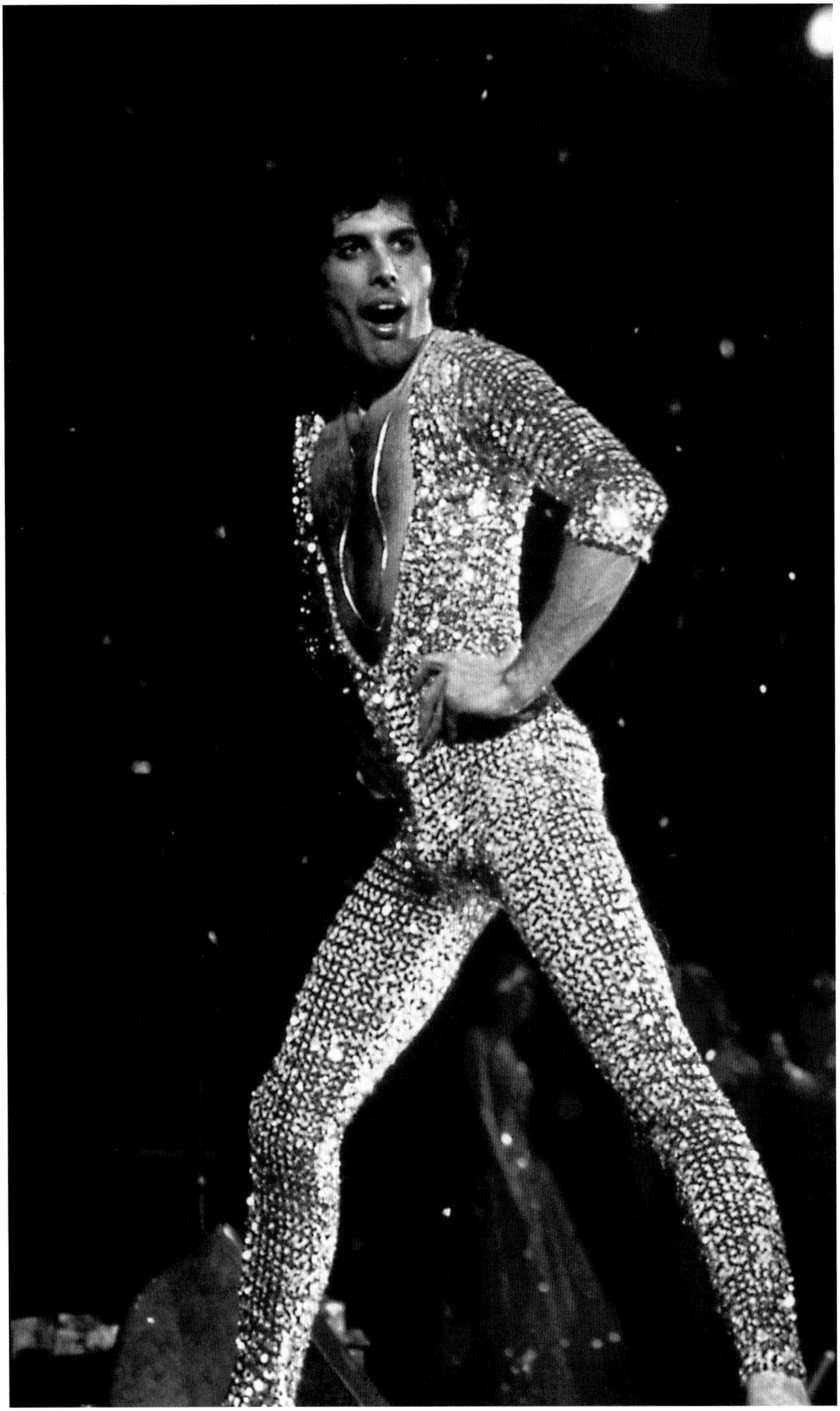

LEFT: Freddie wore the famous sequinned catsuit on tour in 1977…

RIGHT: … and Rami rehearsing in a recreation of the same costume.

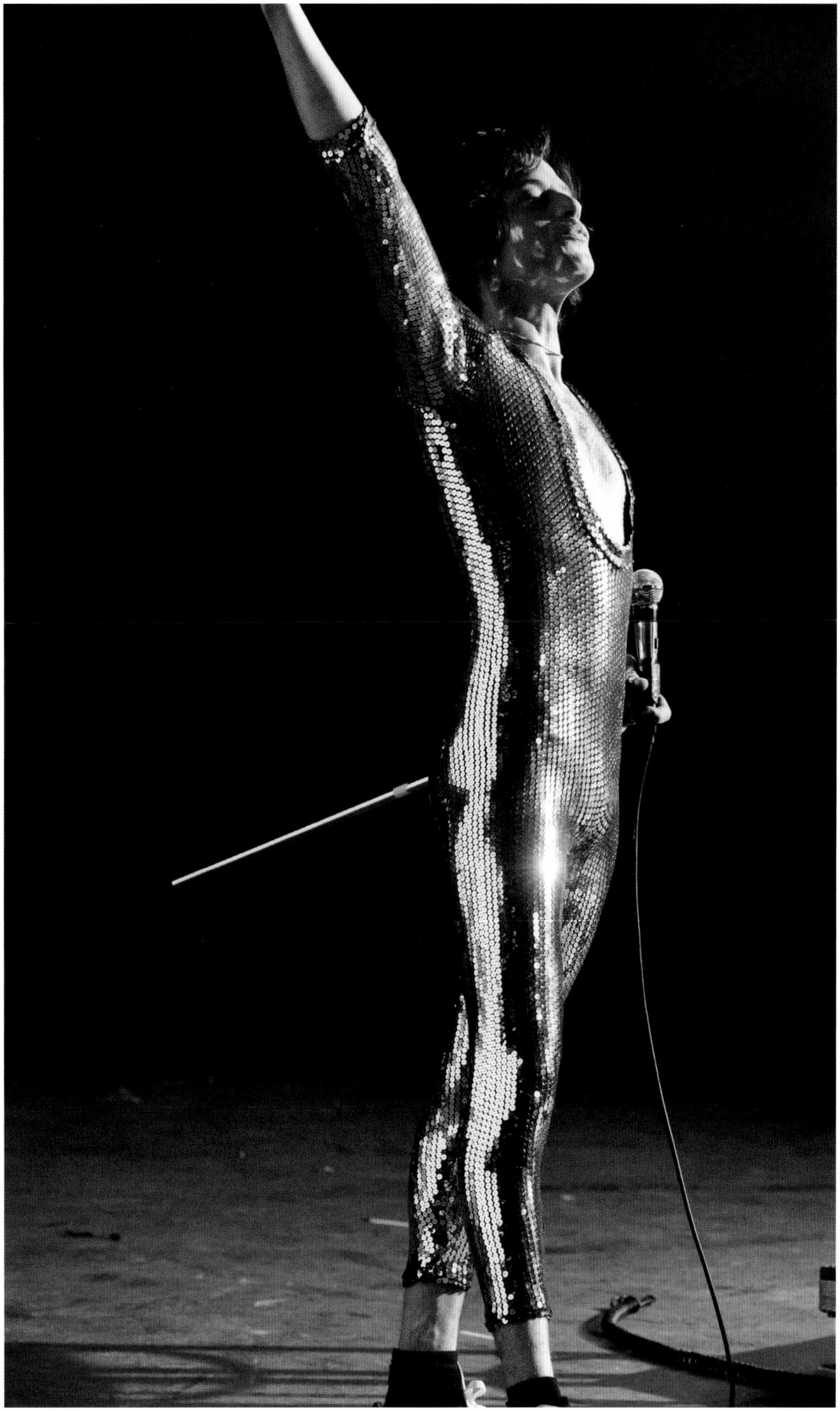

"THERE ARE SO MANY DIFFERENT FACES OF FREDDIE MERCURY, AND I DON'T THINK ONE IS ANY TRUER THAN THE OTHER."

Rami Malek

LEFT: Costume designer Julian Day used William Friedkin's film *Cruising* as a reference for the 1980s New York gay club scene.

BELOW: "Goodbye everybody, it's time to go…" – Rami Malek.

OVERLEAF LEFT: Freddie Mercury's leather look; **and RIGHT:** Rami in leather.

OPPOSITE ABOVE: A thoughtful Gwilym Lee as Brian May. **OPPOSITE BELOW:** Ben Hardy adopts his Roger Taylor disguise. **ABOVE:** Whisky and cigarettes for the John Deacon and Roger Taylor actors on set.

CHAPTER FIVE

THE SHOW MUST GO ON: THE SETS

BOHEMIAN
RHAPSODY
SLATE
68
TAKE
1A
A054
CAM: NEWTON THOMAS SIGEL ASC
04/10/2017

THE STUDIO

Queen recorded their 1975 masterpiece *A Night At The Opera* at several studios, including the idyllic Rockfield complex in Monmouthshire, Wales. Rural, residential facilities like Rockfield and Surrey's Ridge Farm (where they wrote and rehearsed the album) were a perfect way for bands to work in peace and isolation, away from the distractions of London.

For the recording session sequences of the *Bohemian Rhapsody* movie, production designer Aaron Haye opted to take visual inspiration from both Rockfield and Ridge Farm.

"Rockfield still exists as a studio, and there's archive and documentary footage of the band there that was really helpful to us," Haye explains. "But there are also wonderful, iconic photos of the band in this really fantastic environment of Ridge Farm, which was this old converted barn. We scouted several locations and found one that we felt just worked perfectly: this 200-year-old barn with oak beams that we decided would be perfect to build a recording studio in. What we built was sort of an amalgam based on the space and the story we wanted to tell, which was that there was a farmhouse and a guesthouse and a barn and recording studio.

"When we first got there it was filled with horses and hay, and smelled of manure, and all that fun stuff. So we cleared all of that out and designed a space that would allow us to build a 1970s recording studio in this eighteenth century barn and make it feel real. We tried our best to give it that warm 70s feeling. It was another one of the locations that Brian May visited. He actually played a bit of the solo from 'Bohemian Rhapsody' in that space."

One of the earliest analogue albums to be recorded on 24 tracks, *A Night At The Opera* was mixed on a variety of then cutting-edge recording consoles, with 'Bohemian Rhapsody' itself put together on the Trident B. For the film, Haye and his team actually built the recording desk from scratch, scouring photographs for visual references and eventually settling for its look not on Ridge Farm or Rockfield's genuine equipment, but a Neve console that was actually in a different recording studio in 70s Notting Hill.

"It was so iconic and so sort of 70s sci-fi that we fell in love with it," says Haye. "It almost looked like Scotty might beam you up with it. And so that was the one that I decided we would recreate. We made it function to the point where we could actually see each individual track monitoring on it: the console lights all lit. That felt really authentic. There's a wonderful shot that moves over the desk and out into the recording space as Gwilym, playing Brian May, is recording his guitar solo. You get goose bumps watching things like that."

OPPOSITE: Everything was recorded to tape in the 1970s; these were recreated for the movie.

TOP: An engineer watches Brian May (Gwilym Lee) lay down 'Bohemian Rhapsody''s famous solo.

ABOVE: The recreation of SARM studios' Neve console, built for the Ridge Farm studio set.

LEFT: Careful recreation of the studio noticeboard.

ABOVE: The actors around the mic recording 'Bohemian Rhapsody''s intricate harmonies.

OPPOSITE: On the Ridge Farm studio set recreating the recording of 'Bohemian Rhapsody'.

BELOW: LPs in a German music shop in *Bohemian Rhapsody* alongside the original album covers for Queen's *Greatest Hits* and Freddie's *Mr. Bad Guy*.

OVERLEAF: L-R: Rami Malek as Freddie Mercury, Allen Leech as Paul Prenter, Joseph Mazzello as John Deacon, Ben Hardy as Roger Taylor; on the Ridge Farm studio set.

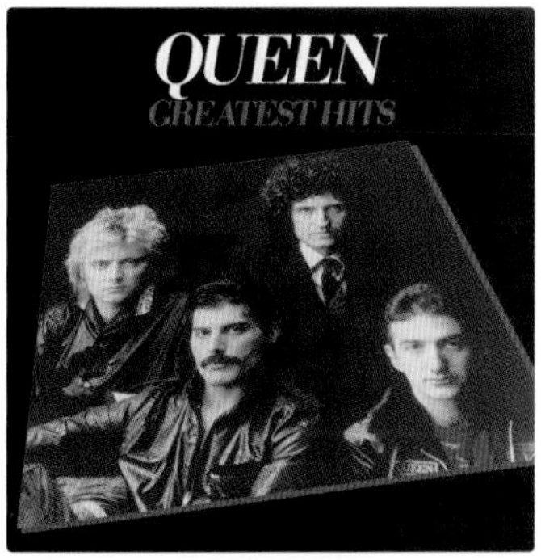

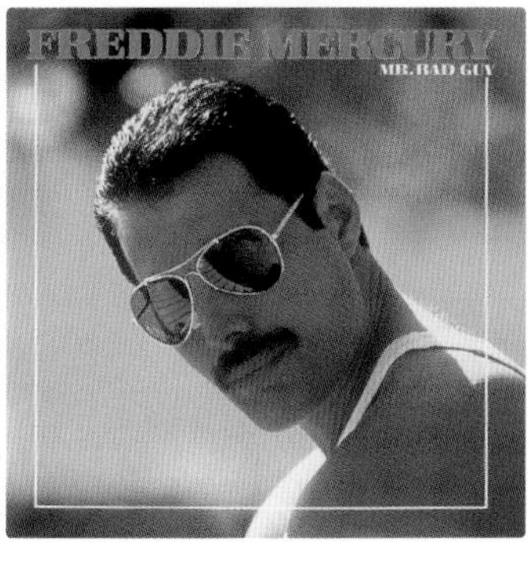

LIVE QUEEN

AWAY FROM THE LIVE AID STAGE RECREATED IN HEMEL HEMPSTEAD, THE SETS FOR THE REST OF *BOHEMIAN RHAPSODY'S* MAJOR CONCERT SEQUENCES WERE HOUSED AT A SINGLE LOCATION AT THE LH2 STUDIOS IN PARK ROYAL, NORTH WEST LONDON.

The huge space has a ground floor area of 1,668.8sq m (17,693sq ft) and a height clearance of 18.1m (60ft), with a rigging grid for lights and other equipment capable of holding in excess of 60 tonnes. Its primary function is as a rehearsal space for bands and musicians preparing for big tours, but it has also been used as a stage for TV shows like *The Voice* and *The X Factor*. With a combination of careful production design, costume and visual effects work, it turned out to be the perfect environment to double for locations from London to New York and from Tokyo to Rio.

"It was quite a bit of work to make one stage look like multiple stages," says Production Designer Aaron Haye. "There was a lot of planning between all the different departments to start redressing for the next stage we needed as soon as one had been completed."

The film depicts the band playing shows from the 70s to the 80s: a period during which there were copious rapid changes to the band's costumes, instruments and makeup, not to mention the fashions worn by their international crowds. But one of the biggest alterations over the years was to the lighting rigs of their stage sets, which grew ever more complex and spectacular as the band rose in stature. "Tom Siegel and his practical stage lighting team really put in the effort there," says Haye. "We had to come up with a way to quickly fly lights in and out and change the colours. We had to use traditional old-school lights rather than contemporary LEDs. The rig that we built over the Madison Square Garden set in particular became referred to as 'the pizza oven', because it would bake you. The front of the stage got pretty hot, but the guys never complained."

Of course, it wouldn't be much of a concert without a crowd, so as much attention had to be paid to the audience as the band onstage if the correct ambience, international culture and period feel was to be achieved. "We start in the UK in the 1970s at Ealing, which was where the band were at college and they played their first gigs," recalls Costume Designer Julian Day. "I wanted quite a hippie, early 70s, Woodstock sort of feel for the audiences at those gigs. The colours were slightly more subdued for Britain at the time.

"Then we go to America in 1974 where they toured as a support group [for Mott the Hoople]. So, that's more Western and suede and fringing, checked shirts and cowboy hats. And then we go to Japan in 75, which we made more colourful and a bit more pop-art. When we hit the 80s we do Rio, which is obviously a South American vibe with a lot more flesh on show. And then we do Madison Square Garden, getting back to New York, which is a different vibe than we did for the American gigs before because it's a bit more ethnically mixed and a bit more street."

And with the physical sets and finite numbers of extras taking the real-world production as far as it could go, it was then the job of the Visual Effects department to travel the remaining distance.

"Most of the action takes place around the stage areas, and the other departments did a really great job with all the lighting and setting up the stage and matching what they did for the real concerts," says Visual Effects Supervisor Paul Norris. "So what we needed to do was create the wider environments. Madison Square Garden is still the same building but it is a little bit different on site now then it was back in 1977, so we had to research that and build a CG asset of the interior. Budokan is a bit more modern now too, although it

ABOVE: Rami as Freddie performing in the Budokan, Japan sequence.

hasn't changed quite so much, but again, we recreated it the way it looked when Queen played there for the first time. There are views where we look out from the stage over the audience, or we look back across the audience at the stage."

To fill in those spaces, Norris employed similar tricks to those used for the Live Aid sequences, shooting as many extras as possible with six cameras, and scanning them to make "digital people" from them if needed. A process known as "podding" was also utilized, where following one take, "we get everybody to jumble up, swap their hats or jackets over or that kind of thing, so they would look a bit different. Then we would move them back into another area and film them again." With only enough extras to populate the space near the front of the stage, all were filmed multiple times in multiple places. When those "plates" are combined in post-production, bolstered by the "digi-crowd", the basic effect of the massive audience is achieved, before being further digitally finessed. "A lot of it is playing around with the lights flashing across the crowd and the spotlights and the ambient light from the stage as the performance is going on," Norris explains. "Plus the other atmospherics like smoke and dry ice and all of the rest of it!"

VOX
VOX

PREVIOUS PAGES: Flamboyant Freddies: **(TOP LEFT):** Rami in red leather on the Madison Square Garden set. **(BOTTOM LEFT):** Freddie performing at Madison Square Garden in 1980. **(RIGHT):** Rami in black leather; a 1974-era costume.

LEFT ABOVE: An early pub gig for the former Smile / newly formed Queen from the movie.

LEFT BELOW: Ben Hardy as Roger at the drum kit.

RIGHT: Queen performed 'Killer Queen' on *Top of the Pops* in 1974; **ABOVE:** The set was recreated for the movie.

GARDEN LODGE

Garden Lodge mansion was Freddie's home from 1980. His "country house in town", it was a secluded, private residence in the Royal Borough of Kensington and Chelsea, hidden by high walls and railings, and nestled within an acre of landscaped gardens, despite only being round the corner from Kensington High Street.

Freddie nonchalantly paid £500,000 for it in cash, boasting that he went from the status of viewer to owner in the space of a mere half an hour. The previous owner had been a member of the Hoare banking family, so it amused Freddie to punningly call it "The Hoare House".

With Mary Austin still living there, it fell to production designer Aaron Haye to find a suitable stand-in house for *Bohemian Rhapsody*. "To find something like that was a real challenge," he says. "It had be on the right scale, and we needed to have enough access to it. So we were lucky to find a house that was relatively unscathed by the film world, and convince the owners to let us use it. They had just bought it and it was completely empty, and I managed to convince them to let us wallpaper and paint and everything as long as we put it back to the way it was originally."

The house needed to be seen in three separate states for different sections of the film: empty and full of boxes for Freddie's moving-in period; in full finished form for the years of Freddie's occupancy; and in a lavishly embellished state for a chaotic party sequence. "And those things didn't necessarily happen in the production order we might have liked," Haye laughs. "That was another part of the challenge."

"We looked at visual archives and took inspiration from the things that we knew Freddie liked, even if we didn't have the exact representation," Haye explains. "Freddie would come back with things from around the world, and there's some great reference of him sitting in a room surrounded by packages from Japan and various things. So we really tried to bring as much of that into his house as we could." In the film as in real life, Freddie's beloved collection of Japanese art sits alongside objects like the porcelain chandeliers he snatched up while on tour in the Eastern Bloc.

As much as visual fidelity is important, however, Haye says that capturing the less quantifiable feel of Garden Lodge during Freddie's lifetime was foremost in everyone's minds. "Peter Freestone [Freddie's personal assistant from 1979 to 1991] spent years with Freddie in that house," he says, "and he came in and told us, 'Yeah, that's it. It may not be exactly the same layout, but this feels like Freddie's house.' That's exactly what we wanted to achieve."

RIGHT: Freddie's Garden Lodge mansion was opulently decorated, including examples of the Japanese art he collected, for this movie recreation.

ABOVE: Garden Lodge on moving-in day in the movie.

BELOW: The actors looking pensive on the Garden Lodge set.

RIGHT: 1980-era Freddie (Rami Malek) at Garden Lodge.

THE PARTY

THERE ARE MANY, MANY TALES OF THE BACCHANALIAN PARTIES THAT FREDDIE MERCURY THREW. SOME OF THE STORIES MAY BE APOCRYPHAL AND WHEN QUIZZED ABOUT THEM, GUESTS TEND TO MAINTAIN A MISCHIEVOUS SILENCE.

Some have spoken of naked girls in painted-on suits serving champagne, or naked living statues in the grounds of Garden Lodge. For his 35th birthday Freddie flew friends to New York on Concorde for a five-day binge. He celebrated his 38th at London's Xenon with 500 friends and a five-foot cake in the shape of a vintage Rolls Royce; his 39th with the famous "black and white drag ball" for 300 flown-in guests at the Munich club Henderson's; his 40th with a giant Mad Hatter's Tea Party at home. It wasn't until his 44th birthday that the pace began to slow and the key began to lower.

Those multiple gaudy nights have, in *Bohemian Rhapsody*, been collated into a single representative event, taking place at Freddie's Garden Lodge mansion. "It's meant to evoke all those occasions," explains Production Designer Aaron Haye. "We have a few genuine details from all those parties, as well as just some things that we felt would tell the story. We had everything from the characters that were there, to massive displays of food and fruit, and gold lions, and two [naked] women on stationary bicycles from the 'Bicycle Race' music video that they'd done. So we tried to touch on a lot of things that either were part of Queen's history or something Freddie was into. We wanted to fill the house with a taste of the debauchery and fun and excess that he was living at that time."

For Freddie's party outfit, Costume Designer Julian Day looked to the black-and-white ball, where he wore "this sort of military jacket and red leather trousers". But the decision was also taken to use this scene to introduce the regal Mercury crown-and-cape ensemble. "In reality he wore that later on, but [narratively] this seemed like a perfect time to introduce it, as if he was king of his own party." Day also describes the dozens of background performers – "drag queens… every type of person imaginable…" – who also had to be dressed appropriately. "We looked at images from Studio 54, or the looks from different nightclubs or the fetish scene of the time, and amalgamated them all."

For Haye, the major concern was to convey the sheer scale of the madness, so he was delighted at the idea of a long travelling shot. "We had an exterior with beautiful luxury cars and vehicles from the late 70s and early 80s," he recalls, "and we wanted to able to come from that front door, with fire-breathers and giants and all these amazing people, and move through and discover Freddie and follow him through the party. It was really wonderful to know that we were going to get to see that in a single take."

OPPOSITE: Rami as Freddie gets the Garden Lodge party started.

PREVIOUS PAGE: "As if he was king of his own party..." (Julian Day, Costume Designer).

ABOVE, BELOW, OVERLEAF: Freddie's opulent parties were legendary, including gifts and champagne for every guest. Many details were carefully recreated for the movie.

OPPOSITE: Freddie Mercury on his 39th birthday.

I WANT TO BREAK FREE

FAITHFULLY RECREATED WITHIN BOHEMIAN RHAPSODY IS QUEEN'S HILARIOUS VIDEO FOR 'I WANT TO BREAK FREE'. THE SONG WAS COMPOSED BY JOHN DEACON FOR THE ALBUM *THE WORKS*, AND RELEASED AS A SINGLE IN APRIL 1984.

It was Roger Taylor's idea for the promo clip to feature the band dressed as women in a parody of the British soap opera *Coronation Street*. "We'd done some epic videos in the past, and we wanted to prove that we didn't take ourselves too seriously," Taylor recalled. Deacon played a grandmother figure; Taylor a schoolgirl; May a glamour-puss with his famous hair in curlers; and Mercury a frustrated, leather-skirted, stocking-clad, large-breasted housewife, lamenting her lot as she pushes a vacuum around her terraced house. The video's director David Mallet convinced Mercury not to shave his moustache for the role.

Here, cast and crew reminisce about the 2018 version…

"The 'I Want To Break Free' video was just a joy to do. It's pretty well documented and we wanted to get as close to that as we possibly could. We were lucky enough to be able to find the exact model of the vacuum cleaner that Freddie's using, and the little light-up alarm clock at the beginning of the video. I think everybody had fun on that set."

Aaron Haye (Production Designer)

"It was really, really good fun. We made a lot of the costumes, but things like Ben's striped socks and the straw boater we found by internet shopping or going out into London to find stuff. We made Gwilym's negligee, and we had some of the cloth and ribbons dyed the right colour."

Julian Day (Costume Designer)

"One of the great things about being an actor is getting to do the most bizarre things, and getting to dress up like four women from *Coronation Street*, and re-enact the Queen 'I Want to Break Free' video was something I'll remember for a long time. It was a very surreal day, and very funny, dressing up as a schoolgirl, as Roger did. I don't think I was as pretty as Roger. Roger made a very pretty schoolgirl."

Ben Hardy

"I think that we all thought that Ben would look a lot better in a dress than he did. We felt he was a little too muscular for us. Rami's moustache I think really works. Keeping that was a really beautiful touch by Freddie Mercury. And I'm glad that Rami got to vacuum for us. It was wild. It was easily one of the most fun and memorable days on set. It was hard to keep a straight face. It was hard to be serious. And it was only fitting that I would finally be able to bring that side of me out and let the world see it."

Joseph Mazzello

OPPOSITE Rami as Freddie in the recreation of the 'I Want to Break Free' video shoot.

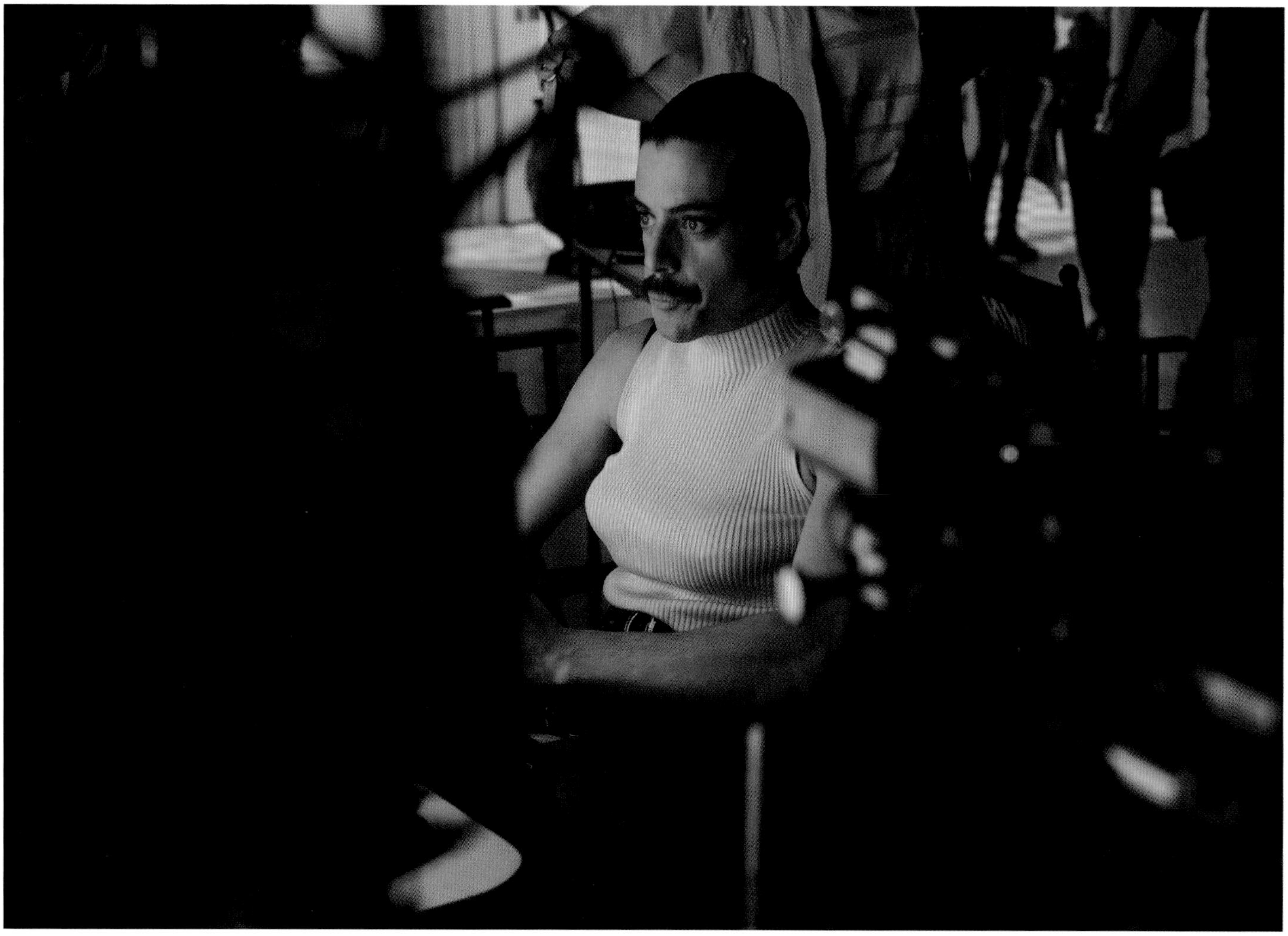

ABOVE: Freddie saw the comedy value in keeping his moustache for his drag performance; Rami followed suit.

BELOW: Movie in a movie: the recreated clapperboard from the video.

BELOW RIGHT: Roger Taylor on set of the original shoot of 'I Want to Break Free'.

OPPOSITE: "I don't think I was as pretty as Roger." – Ben Hardy.

OVERLEAF: Rami (right) and Freddie (left) dressed alike.

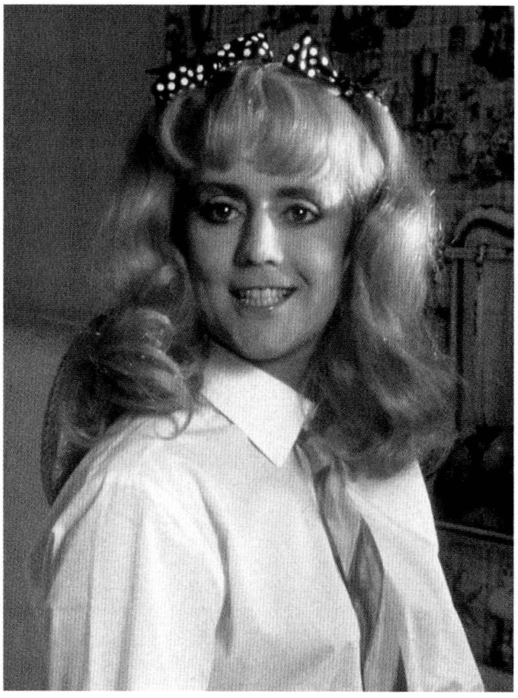

HOOVER

"IT WAS EASILY ONE OF THE MOST FUN AND MEMORABLE DAYS ON SET."

Joseph Mazzello

LIVE AID

"Queen were absolutely the best band of the day. Whatever your personal taste was irrelevant. When the day came they played the best, they had the best sound, they used their time to the full. They understood the idea exactly. They just went and smashed out one hit after the other. It was just unbelievable. I was actually upstairs in the appeals box in Wembley Stadium, and suddenly I heard this sound. I thought, 'God, who's this?'. I went outside and saw that it was Queen. I looked down over this crowd of people just going crazy, and the band were amazing. I think they were delighted afterwards – Freddie in particular. It was the perfect stage for him: the whole world."

Bob Geldof (*Mojo*, August 1999)

ABOVE: Roger Taylor, Bob Geldof and Brian May on the movie's Live Aid set.

RIGHT: Recreating Live Aid.

LIVE
AID
412L
QUEEN

Ethiopia was dying. Horrified by the pictures of starving children he was seeing on the news every day, Boomtown Rats singer Bob Geldof took it upon himself to organize the biggest charity concert the world had ever seen, to raise funds for the relief effort. Live Aid took place on July 13, 1985, at the UK's Wembley Stadium and the John F. Kennedy Stadium in Pennsylvania, USA, with subsidiary concerts in Australia, Austria, Canada, Japan, the Soviet Union, the former Yugoslavia and West Germany. Dozens of the world's biggest musical acts performed sets throughout the extraordinary day. Broadcast globally via satellite link-ups, the event was watched on television by an estimated 40 per cent of the world's population, raising at least £50m for its cause.

Live Aid was a make-or-break opportunity for Queen, and a moment that they seized. Personally and professionally the band had not been at its strongest in recent times. The combination of the curveball *Hot Space* album and the cross-dressing video for 'I Want To Break Free' had seen their American audience dwindle catastrophically. And while they had never been fashionable – their mainstream success came with a broader audience riding out trends like punk and new-wave – they were beginning to viewed less favourably in the politically conscious 80s, thanks to their questionable decision to ignore a cultural boycott and play concerts in Apartheid-riven South Africa. They had not been invited to participate in the 'Do They Know It's Christmas' charity single by Band Aid; a supergroup collection of younger, trendier stars.

When it came to Live Aid, however, Geldof was keen to appeal to as broad a worldwide viewing spectrum as possible. He wanted the classics acts, and even though their stock was falling, having Queen involved was a no-brainer.

ABOVE: Rami Malek prepares to take to the stage as Freddie at Live Aid.

For the purposes of *Bohemian Rhapsody*'s movie narrative, Live Aid has been portrayed as Queen's reunion after Mercury departed for a solo career. In real life, Mercury's solo project happened alongside Queen's normal schedule, and the band was still very much active, having recently completed a tour of Australia, New Zealand and Japan. Geldof approached the band through Jim Beach, but his invitation wasn't immediately or enthusiastically received. It was only when the sheer size of the event was impressed upon them that the band, and particularly Mercury, realized its potential and agreed to take part.

Queen gave it their all, reminding the world just how great they could be at the top of their game. Queen "got" the format. They understood that Live Aid was a "global jukebox", and opted to pummel through a series of their most recognizable hits in their tight 20-minute slot, rather than try to showcase new material. And while other bands busked and winged it, the infamously perfectionist Queen's set was meticulously rehearsed for weeks in advance. It was absolutely the right decision. They began with Mercury taking to the piano for the early part of 'Bohemian Rhapsody', and continued to motor through 'Radio Ga Ga', 'Hammer To Fall', 'Crazy Little Thing Called Love' and 'We Will Rock You', before ending on a triumphal 'We Are The Champions'. Mercury was in his element, all over the stage and owning it in front of a packed Wembley crowd of 72,000 people – who he found time to lead in one of his famous "Ayyyyy-oh!" call-and-response interludes – and a global television audience estimated at two billion. They were also the loudest band of the day, thanks to some sneaky behind-the-scenes manipulation of the sound system's limiters by their engineer James "Trip" Khalaf.

Live Aid was not a competition, but Queen unquestionably won it. To this day, that 20 minutes is regularly hailed as the greatest rock performance of all time.

ABOVE LEFT: Brian May's original Live Aid backstage pass.

ABOVE RIGHT: Freddie and Brian rock Live Aid; **LEFT and RIGHT:** The guitars from the movie scene.

LEFT: Photographers scramble for the perfect image of Brian May (Gwilym Lee) at Live Aid.

ABOVE: Focus on Joseph Mazzello (playing John Deacon) while Rami as Freddie plays piano in the foreground.

BELOW: Ben Hardy dwarfed by Roger Taylor's drum kit. Taylor was on hand to make sure it was set up correctly.

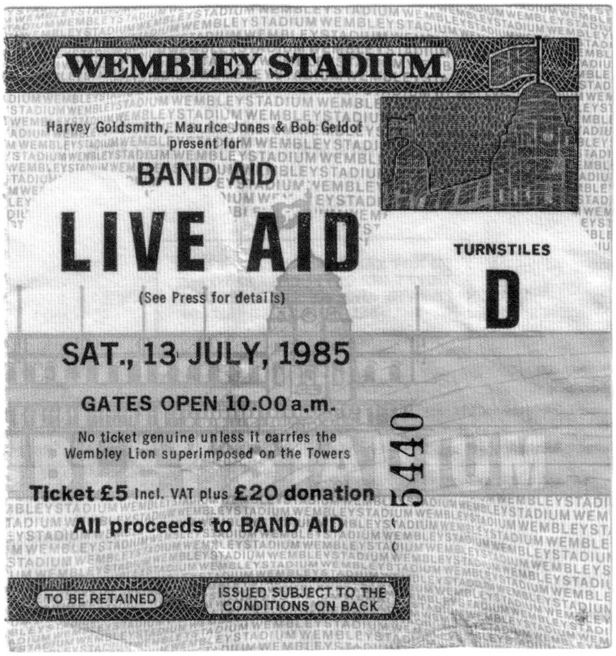

ABOVE: Live Aid tickets cost £25 – 80 per cent of which went to famine relief in Ethiopia.

RIGHT: Movie recreation of the outside broadcast unit.

BELOW RIGHT: Cover of the original Live Aid souvenir programme.

BELOW: Queen's now-legendary Live Aid setlist, recreated for the movie.

OPPOSITE: "Aaaaaaaaaay-oh!" Rami / Freddie points the mic outwards for some audience participation.

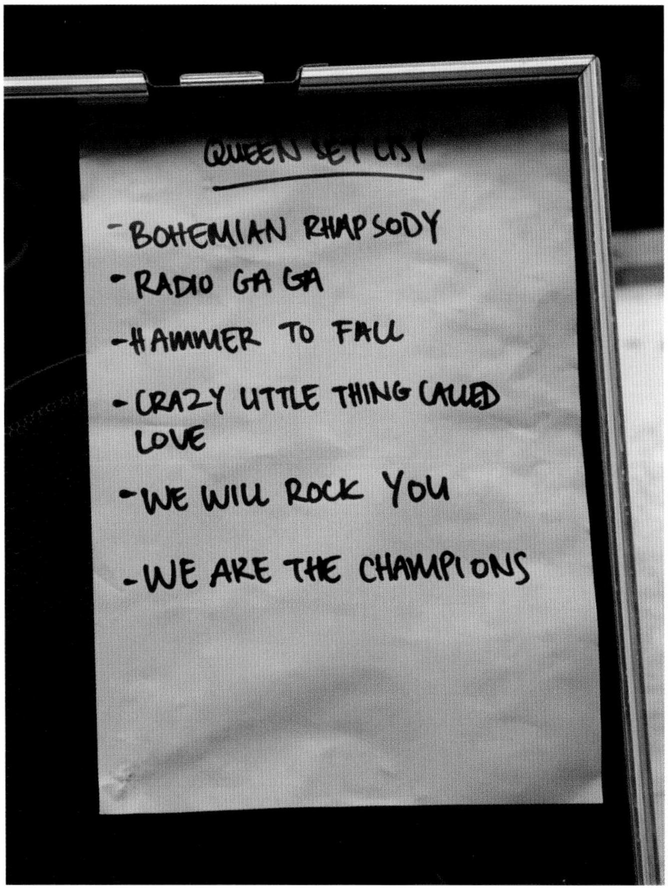

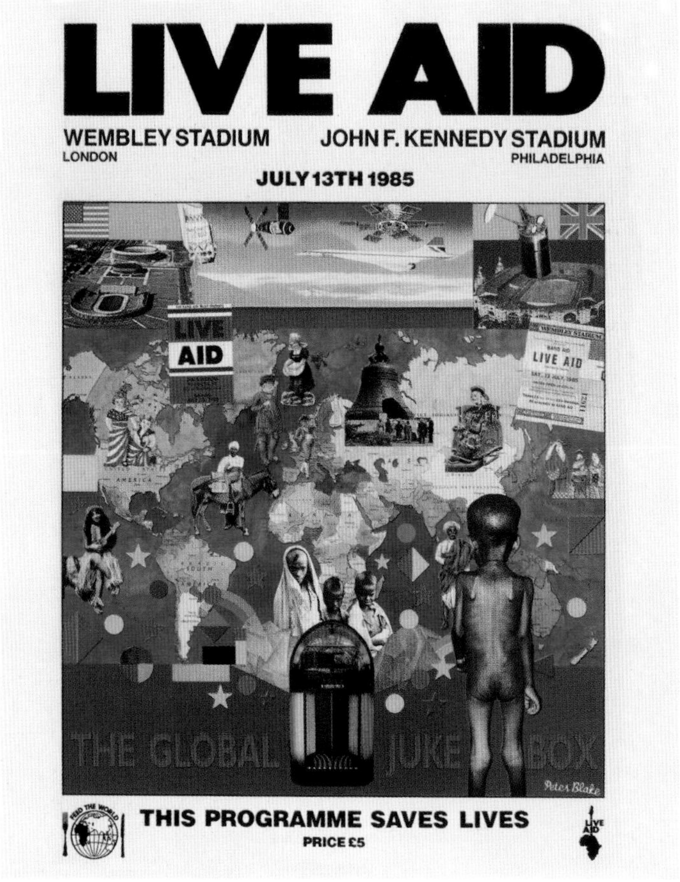

QUEEN

LIVE AID – VFX

RECREATING LIVE AID BEGAN DURING THE FIRST WEEK OF *BOHEMIAN RHAPSODY*'S PRODUCTION, WITH AN EXACT REPLICA OF THE WEMBLEY LIVE AID STAGE CREATED AT BOVINGDON AIRFIELD NEAR HEMEL HEMPSTEAD…

Of course, it wasn't enough just to build the stage. Production designer Aaron Haye and his team did a spectacular job of physically matching the space on which Queen actually performed at Live Aid, but the job of recreating the rest of Wembley Stadium as it was in 1985, not to mention populating it with 72,000 people, was that of the Visual Effects department.

"Beyond the stage is just an airfield in Bovington," laughs Visual Effects Supervisor Chris Norris. "My department needed to cover up what's really there and create [with CGI] everything that hadn't been built. We've obviously had to do a lot of archival research and watch a lot of Live Aid footage to break down all the elements we needed."

One of the biggest challenges was the fact that the enormous artificial crowd actually had to perform convincingly along with the band on stage. There were Mercury's call-and-response antics to be considered; the hand-clapping movements that crowds to this day contribute to 'Radio Ga Ga'; the clapping and stomping that goes with 'We Will Rock You', and so on.

Norris and his crew achieved this by setting up a separate shoot away from their main Live Aid stage, and filming around 120 extras over and over again. "We would take them one at a time and film them simultaneously on six cameras," he explains. "We had a video feed or archive footage where they could see what the performance would be, and it was kind of like a karaoke-type situation where they could watch what they were being asked to do. It ended up as a very efficient system of getting someone in, get them to go through each of these different actions, which took about 15 minutes for each person, and then move them out and get the next one in. And do the same. Over and over again. For five consecutive days!"

The advantage of this laborious technique is that, rather than populate their Wembley with digital mannequins, the crowd will be made up of genuine people. "It brings a photo-real feel to the whole thing," Haye continues. "We will replicate that 120 people thousands of times, and to stop that being obvious we can use little tricks like changing the colour of their clothes or hair, or their skin tone. Having filmed them on six cameras, from six angles, we can actually move them around slightly in three dimensions, so we can get some of the simpler camera moves around them. And we have a system whereby we can tell the software to put in a certain percentage of people who are just doing generic things, because not everybody was joining in, let's be honest. That matters because you have to make it seem real. If every single person in that hundred-thousand crowd is doing exactly the same thing, it looks fake, so you have to mix it up."

RIGHT: The life-sized recreation of the Live Aid set at Bovingdon.

FEED THE WORLD
JULY 13th 1985 at WEMBLEY STADIUM
LIVE AID
LIVE AID

FEED THE WORLD
JULY 13th 1985 at WEMBLEY STADIUM
LIVE AID
LIVE AID
LIVE AID
LIVE AID

LIVE AID
NO ALCOH
BEYOND
THIS POIN
73KG
QUEEN
5
Queen
QUEEN
YEL-5
MIX

"We started with the hardest thing first. There are no blueprints, for whatever reason, for Wembley at the time, so we had to rely on reference from photographs and documentary footage and figure out how we were going to build it. We got in touch with the same company that built the original scaffolding, so a couple of the gentlemen that were there on the day in 1985, amazingly enough, were there with us building that."

Aaron Haye (Production Designer)

"The stage set for Live Aid was very purposely sort of austere. The event was meant to raise money for Ethiopia, and so the last thing that the promoters wanted to do was spend a lot of money on a big, fancy stage. So inherently, you have an undramatic set, and undramatic lighting, and yet you want it to be your climatic scene and show one of the greatest performances in rock history. The thing that we had going for it is that Queen were fortunate enough to play as the sun was setting, so we see a progression from flatter daylight to, by the time they get to 'We Are the Champions', the artificial lighting of the stage taking on more importance."

Newton Thomas Sigel (Cinematographer)

"We really wanted to be able to tell the Live Aid story going from the dressing room from Freddie's arrival, through the backstage area and out onto the stage and the reaction of the crowd. It was quite an endeavor to squeeze all that in. In reality, the backstage was a bunch of trailers that were outside of the stadium. What we decided to do was to bring a bit of that backstage trailer feel into the stadium itself so that we could tell that story more efficiently."

Aaron Haye

"Bob Geldof came out and stood on that stage and got very emotional. It felt right, as soon as we started rehearsing. It kind of transformed all of us. There was so much energy in that week that we were creating something very special."

Graham King

"Starting the production with Live Aid was madness. It was so full-on, not only in terms of the musical challenge of learning all those songs, but we also had to try and look like a band that have been together for years."

Gwilym Lee (Brian May)

"It was daunting. Brian May showed up for one of the Live Aid rehearsals before we knew how to play the songs and we had to fake it. We had to fake Brian May songs in front of Brian May!"

Joseph Mazzello (John Deacon)

"The opportunity to play the whole set in one go was a bit like the difference between doing theatre and film: you actually play the journey of that gig and you understand the momentum of the day."

Gwilym Lee

"Doing it three or four times in a row was a pretty exhausting experience, but it was great. Roger watched our rehearsal, and he was like, 'Oh wow, did we really play that fast?' And I was like, 'Yes, you bloody did, and I've only been learning this for six weeks!'"

Ben Hardy (Roger Taylor)

LEFT ABOVE: Setting up the Live Aid stage at Bovingdon. **LEFT BELOW:** Queen's recreated equipment backstage on the Live Aid set.

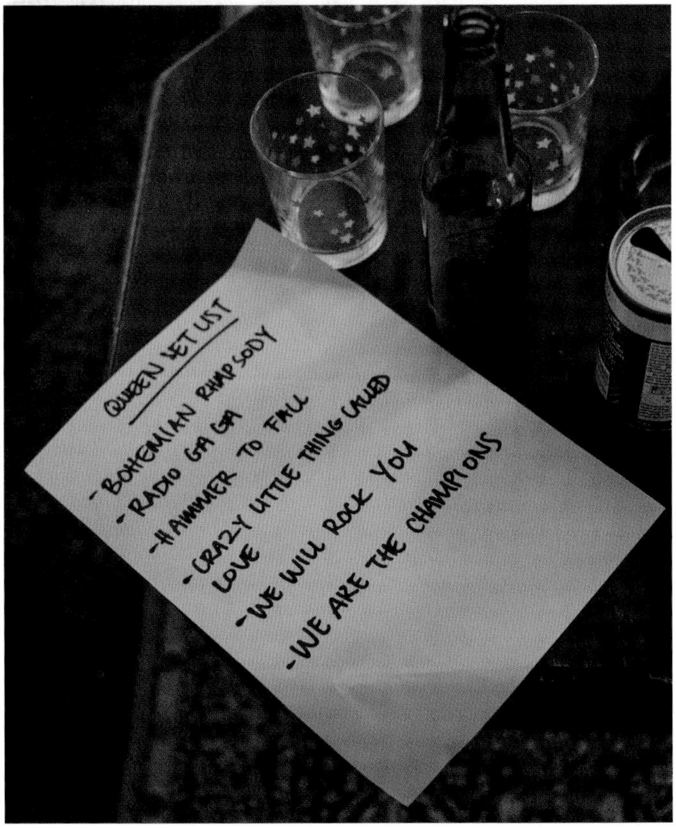

TOP AND OPPOSITE ABOVE: The recreated backstage hospitality area at Live Aid, eerily quiet.

ABOVE: The backstage at Live Aid set, looking busier when filled with actors.

RIGHT: Queen's compact Live Aid set list – a movie prop recreated from the real thing.

OPPOSITE BELOW: The empty stage, waiting for the hammer to fall….

FEED THE WORLD
JULY 13th 1985 at WEMBLEY STADIUM
LIVE AID

BOHEMIAN RHAPSODY

CHAPTER
SIX

WE WILL ROCK YOU: THE MUSIC

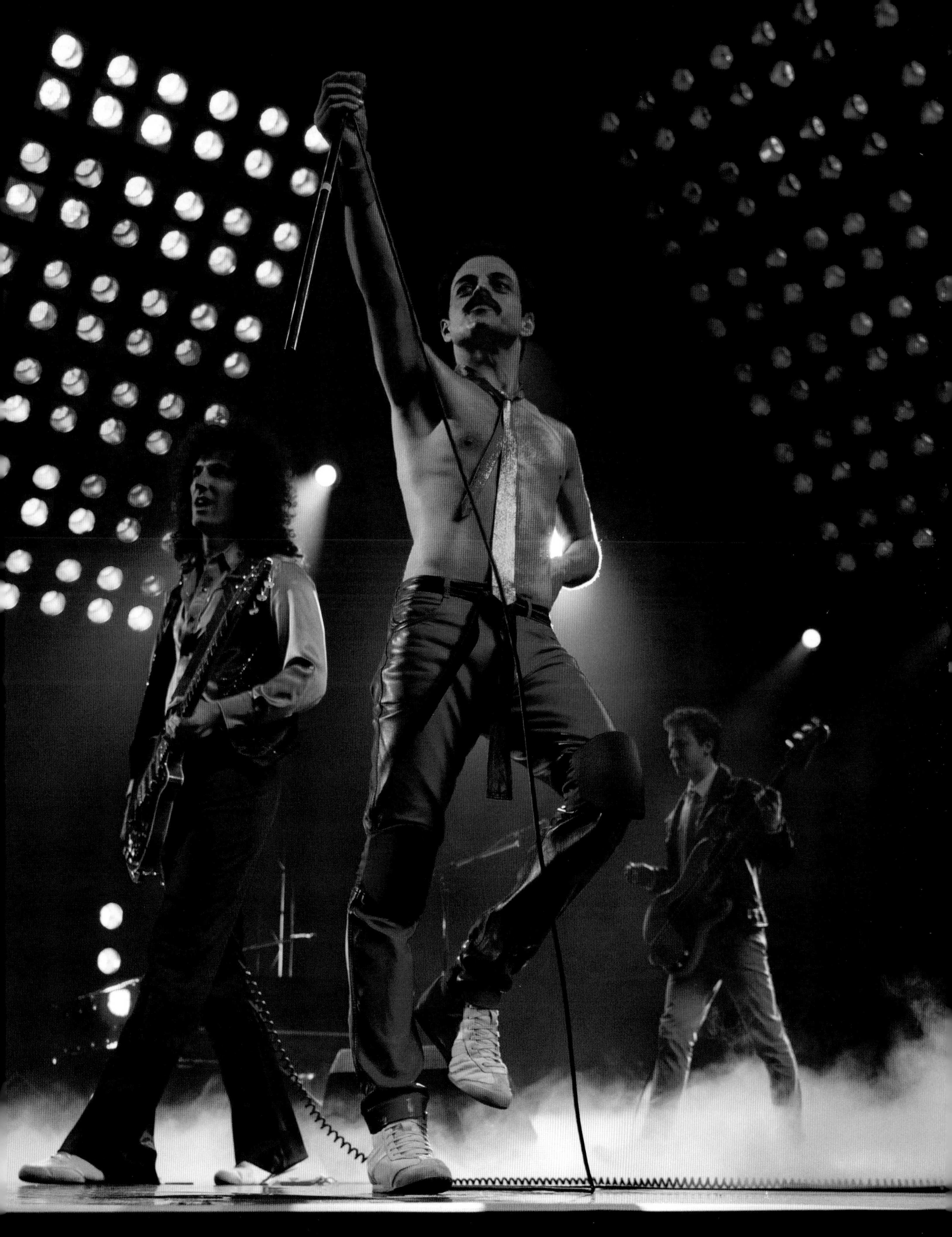

PRESENTING THE MUSIC

WITH TYPICAL FORESIGHT, QUEEN BEGAN CAREFULLY PRESERVING THEIR MUSICAL LEGACY VERY EARLY IN THEIR CAREER. NOT ONLY DID THEY KEEP ALL THE CONSTITUENT PARTS OF THEIR LABORIOUSLY CONSTRUCTED STUDIO TRACKS: THEY ALSO UNDERTOOK THE UNUSUAL (AND UNUSUALLY EXPENSIVE) PROJECT OF PROFESSIONALLY RECORDING MANY OF THEIR LIVE CONCERTS – EVEN IF THERE WAS NO PARTICULAR PLAN TO RELEASE A LIVE ALBUM OF THE SET.

That is, of course, a gift to the *Bohemian Rhapsody* team. "We realized that we had all this incredibly well recorded material to work with," says Supervising Music Editor John Warhurst. "Even live, each instrument – all the drums, the bass, the guitars, everything – was recorded separately and well. All this material is still completely useable in 2018, including Freddie's vocals and all the backing vocals."

Among many other benefits behind the scenes, this particularly helps the film's montage sequences, which might segue from the band recording a song in the studio or performing it on a television show, to playing the same song on stage in front of thousands. "Queen's archive meant we could pull off those transitions quite seamlessly," explains Warhurst. "Where a single performance of, say, 'Fat Bottomed Girls' wouldn't have been enough, we have multiple versions that we can move through."

Replicating Queen's performances physically, meanwhile, was obviously a job for the actors – and a tough one at that. "They come from positions of not really being musicians," Warhurst explains. "But Gwilym, for example, not only has to be able to play like a guitarist, but pass himself off as one of the world's most virtuoso guitarists. To get to that point so quickly is pretty phenomenal. It was the same for Ben. He was worried that he might need a hand double for some of his close-up drum work, but by the time we got to Live Aid he'd practiced so much he could even do all Roger's really complicated stuff with no problem."

With the main focus of the film on Freddie Mercury, Rami Malek was understandably apprehensive too, but again, with hard work and phenomenal perseverance with vocal and movement coaches, he soon gained confidence.

"Freddie sang with a hundred-and-ten-per-cent energy every single time, even on songs that you'd think are more laid back, like 'I Want to Break Free'," says Warhurst. "You could see that Rami was slightly nervous at first, but fast-forward six or seven hours and he didn't want to stop! I think by the end of the first day we probably had about 150 takes and he was still asking if we needed more."

Music Supervisor Becky Bentham explains that it's very important that an actor genuinely "sings out any time he's being filmed, so that he looks authentic in his performance with his throat moving in the right way, his facial muscles all moving in the right way, and so on. But even for a scene like the one where he's composing 'Crazy Little Thing Called Love' in the bathtub… just being able to do that naturally when you're not a natural musician, and the work that it has taken him to become that person, is a huge credit to him."

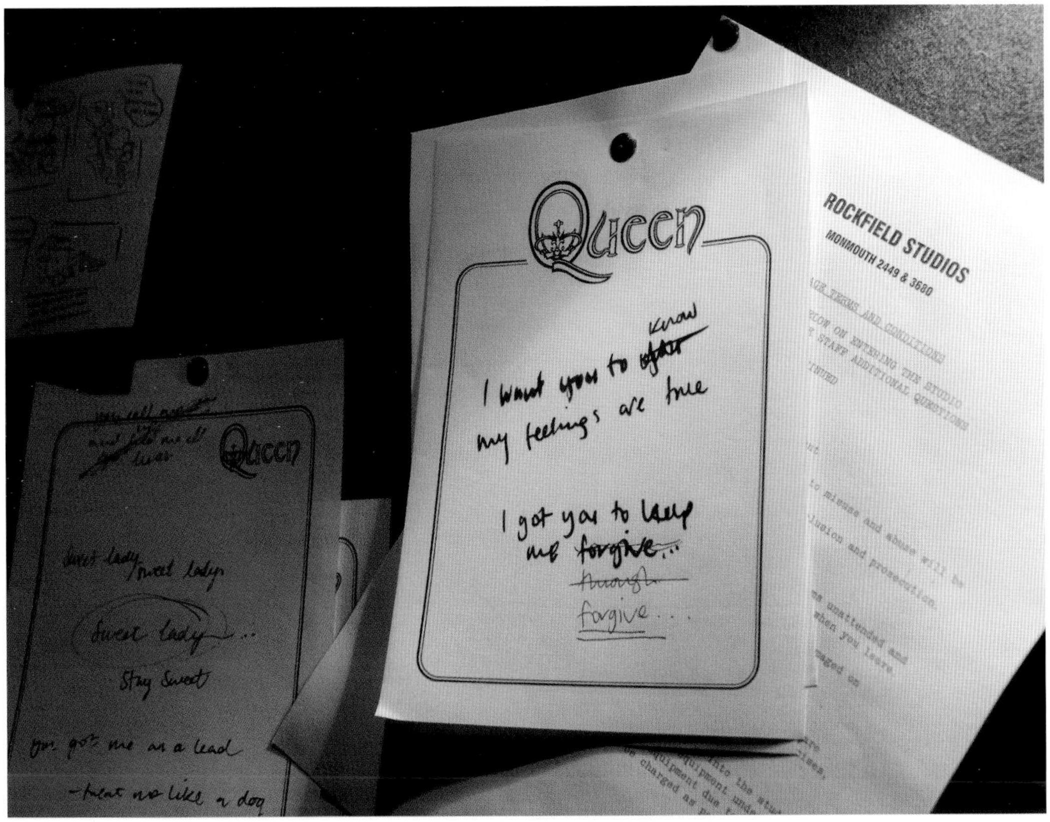

LEFT: Handwritten lyrics to 'You're My Best Friend' – on official Queen stationery, recreated for the movie.

BELOW: You can never have too many guitars and amps on set.

OVERLEAF: Equipment was carefully researched and recreated for the Ridge Farm set, and for the rest of the movie.

TEAC
STUDIONIRE

"BOHEMIAN RHAPSODY"

The song 'Bohemian Rhapsody' is Queen in a nutshell: a showcase of different musical styles in a multi-part, six-minute odyssey taking in piano ballad, crunchy rock riffing and faux operatics. The centrepiece of the *A Night At The Opera* album (even though May's prog epic 'The Prophet's Song' is even longer), it was released as a single three weeks before the album, on October 31, 1975. At the time, it was the most expensive single ever recorded.

The song was composed and conceived by Freddie Mercury, who began working on it long before rehearsals and recording sessions for the album. Freddie knew it wasn't "real" opera, but as an opera fan he wanted to get as close to it as his abilities would allow. Recording began at Rockfield Studios in Monmouthshire, Wales, before moving to SARM in Notting Hill, London: a sophisticated 24-track set up where the difficult vocal arrangements were finished. Creating the effect of the choir from three voices (John Deacon didn't sing on the track, although he mimed for the video) necessitated 200 overdubs and took three weeks to achieve. The middle section changed and grew as the process went on: it was originally only envisaged as a quick 30-second interlude.

Freddie refused to explain the opaque lyrics, which pinball from "Bismillah" (Arabic for "In the name of God") to Scaramouche (a clown in the Italian commedia dell'arte) to Galileo (the scientific genius of the Italian Renaissance). Some thought it an essentially meaningless stream-of-consciousness. Some take the song at face value: a Faustian story about a murderer making his confession. Freddie called it a "fantasy" and said that literally understanding it wasn't important.

'Bohemian Rhapsody' and *A Night At The Opera* came at a make-or-break moment for Queen, when the band was in debt and battling their management. It seemed almost self-destructive to release it as single, when the received wisdom was that a song needed to be half the length to get played on the radio. EMI wanted 'You're My Best Friend' as the album's flagship instead.

In the end it was Capital Radio's maverick DJ Kenny Everett who came to the rescue, championing 'Bohemian Rhapsody' by playing an advance copy multiple times (fourteen in two days!) before the record was even pressed. The resultant mania for the song sent Queen stratospheric. *A Night At The Opera* stayed on the album charts for a year. The affectionately nicknamed 'Bo Rhap' itself stayed at No.1 on the singles chart for nine weeks and had sold a million copies by January 1976.

Unable to play it live – or at least replicate its extravagant mid-section – Queen compromised in concert by playing just the beginning and end sections. For television, they made a promotional film so that *Top of the Pops* and its ilk had something to show. In 1975 its £4,500 cost was an unusually large expense, but on top of all its other achievements, 'Bohemian Rhapsody' ended up accidentally pioneering the art of the music video, which would become ubiquitous in the 1980s thanks to TV channels like MTV and VH1. The song went to No.1 in the UK again when re-released after Freddie's death and in the wake of its famous use in *Wayne's World* in 1991. It's the only song in history to have been the UK Christmas No.1 twice.

RIGHT: Recreating the studio recording of the 'Bohemian Rhapsody' single for the movie.

THE SONGS

BOHEMIAN RHAPSODY IS A HISTORY OF QUEEN'S MUSIC AS WELL AS THE BAND MEMBERS THEMSELVES. FROM DOZENS OF POTENTIALS, THE FOLLOWING 20 TRACKS WERE THE ONES SELECTED BY THE PRODUCTION TO REPRESENT THE BAND'S MUSICAL JOURNEY AND HERITAGE.

KEEP YOURSELF ALIVE
(1973)

Queen's first official single was also the first track on their first album. It received next to no radio airplay and failed to chart, but did attract some favourable attention when played on the BBC music show *The Old Grey Whistle Test*.

SEVEN SEAS OF RHYE
(1974)

Queen's third single and first major hit began life as an instrumental on the first Queen album, before being reworked with typically obscure Mercury lyrics for *Queen II*. It landed them their first appearance on *Top of the Pops*.

PREVIOUS PAGES: The actors recreate Queen's classic photo shoot (**LEFT**) and a shot from the original (**RIGHT**).
RIGHT: Freddie and Brian (Rami and Gwilym) perform together early in their career – in the movie.

KILLER QUEEN
(1974)

Queen's first major hit internationally was taken from their third album, *Sheer Heart Attack*. It was a turning point for the band musically too: a piece of idiosyncratic camp that proved they were more than a hard rock group. Freddie liked to compare it to the music of the film *Cabaret* and the work of Noel Coward.

YOU'RE MY BEST FRIEND
(1975)

A composition by bass player John Deacon, taken from the album *A Night At The Opera*. Deacon wrote the lyrics about his wife, Veronica Tetzlaff. This was the follow-up single to 'Bohemian Rhapsody', reaching the top 10 in the UK and the top 20 in the US.

RIGHT: Roger Taylor, as played by Ben Hardy.

LOVE OF MY LIFE
(1975)

Mercury contributed this heartfelt ballad to the *A Night At The Opera* album. An acoustic live version was released as a single in 1979. The song is generally thought to be about Mary Austin, although some have suggested it was for his then-boyfriend David Minns.

I'M IN LOVE WITH MY CAR
(1975)

An eccentric composition by Roger Taylor for *A Night At The Opera*, 'I'm In Love With My Car' is, as the title suggests, about a man with a feel for his automobile. Supposedly a satire of roadie Jonathan Harris, Brian May believes it was autobiographical for the petrol head Taylor. "He'll tell you it's about someone else, but we know the truth…"

RIGHT: Leather-look Freddie Mercury, as portrayed by Rami Malek.

SOMEBODY TO LOVE
(1976)

Taken from the album *A Day At The Races*, this single utilized similar vocal layering techniques to 'Bohemian Rhapsody', here achieving the effect of a gospel choir. Mercury had legendary soul singer Aretha Franklin in mind when he wrote it.

WE ARE THE CHAMPIONS
(1977)

From the album *News of the World*, this massive anthem was intended by Freddie as his own version of 'My Way', and as a song for the football terraces. It worked; to this day fans spontaneously break into this song at sporting events the world over.

RIGHT: Brian, Roger and Freddie as played by Gwilym, Ben and Rami.

WE WILL ROCK YOU
(1977)

Released as a double A-side with 'We Are the Champions', Brian May wrote the stomp-and-clap classic 'We Will Rock You' specifically for fans to join in with at Queen gigs. It later gave its name to Queen's blockbuster stage musical.

FAT BOTTOMED GIRLS
(1978)

Another Brian May song, and another double A-side single, paired with Mercury's 'Bicycle Race'. The lyrics of both songs reference each other. The cheeky video for the latter featured nude female models cycling around Wimbledon Stadium. This is the English seaside-postcard, '*Carry On*' side of the band.

RIGHT: A recreated set list from the movie.

QUEEN SET LIST [REVISED]
1 PROCESSION
2 FATHER TO SON
3 FAT BOTTOMED GIRLS
4 WHITE QUEEN (AS IT BEGAN)
5 GREAT KING RAT
6 HANGMAN
7 DOING ALL RIGHT
8 SON & DAUGHTER
9 KEEP YOURSELF ALIVE
10 SEVEN SEAS OF RYE
11 LIAR
12 JAILHOUSE ROCK
(PRESLEY COVER)
13 SHAKE RATTLE + ROLL
(BIG JOE TURNER + BLUES
14 STUPID CUPID
(CONNIE FRANCIS
15 JAILHOUSE
16 BIG
17
TIMES ROCK'

DON'T STOP ME NOW
(1978)

Like 'Fat Bottomed Girls' and 'Bicycle Race', this was taken from the album *Jazz*. It wasn't a hit in the US, but research polls and scientific studies have identified as one of the top feel-good songs of all time, and one of the songs that drivers are most likely to break the speed limit to.

CRAZY LITTLE THING CALLED LOVE
(1980)

Mercury boasted that he wrote this belting Elvis-tribute from the album *The Game* in about ten minutes. He was also pleased to have composed it on the guitar, "which I can't play for nuts." He played acoustic rhythm guitar on the song in concert; the first time he ever played guitar live.

RIGHT: Freddie Mercury famously wrote 'Crazy Little Thing Called Love' while in the bath. The scene is recreated in the movie.

ANOTHER ONE BITES THE DUST
(1980)

Queen's biggest hit worldwide – bigger outside the UK even than 'Bohemian Rhapsody' – was a John Deacon composition, pointing the way to a more disco/funk sound for Queen. It sold more than seven million singles.

UNDER PRESSURE
(1981)

Only Queen's second No.1 hit in the UK, this collaboration with David Bowie was the result of a single impromptu 24-hour recording session at the band's Montreux studio. John Deacon's bass riff provided the bedrock, but unusually the song is credited to all the band members.

RIGHT: John Deacon, as played by Joseph Mazzello.

BODY LANGUAGE
(1982)

The first Queen single to feature no guitars at all, this, like the *Hot Space* album it came from, was an attempt to further explore the dance/disco direction of 'Another One Bites The Dust'.

RADIO GA GA
(1984)

A triumphant return, this crowd-pleaser led the album *The Works*, and reached a respectable No.2 in the UK charts and the top 20 in the US. Drummer Roger Taylor wrote it, inspired by the babbling of his baby son.

RIGHT: The movie's recreation of Queen's famous *Hot Space* press conference.

QUEEN

I WANT TO BREAK FREE
(1984)

Another single from *The Works*, credited to John Deacon. It was a major hit all over the world, apart from in America. Its comedic video, in which the band members dressed as women, was refused airplay on MTV.

HAMMER TO FALL
(1984)

Yet another single from *The Works*, 'Hammer To Fall' is a muscular Brian May composition. Failing to reach the UK top 10, it was seen as something of a disappointment, but became a live favourite, even making the set at Live Aid.

RIGHT: Gwilym Lee as Brian May with his trusty Red Special guitar.

WHO WANTS TO LIVE FOREVER
(1986)

Brian May wrote this ballad for the fantasy movie *Highlander*. In the film it plays over a montage of the immortal hero staying physically the same as his wife grows old. In light of Mercury's illness, however, the song took on a poignant second meaning.

THE GREAT PRETENDER
(1987)

A hit for Freddie Mercury solo, this was a cover version of a 1955 song by the Platters. Mercury took a wry liking to the lyrics about a man with a bulletproof public persona who's more vulnerable on the inside.

RIGHT: Rami as Freddie.

PICTURE CREDITS

The publishers would like to thank the following sources for their kind permission to reproduce the pictures in this book.

All images: **Alex Bailey/© Fox** except for the following:

Page 6: Yoshiko Horta/© Queen Productions Ltd; 7: Richard Creamer/Michael Ochs Archives/Getty Images; 23: Pictorial Press Ltd/Alamy; 29: Neal Preston/© Queen Productions Ltd; 31: Douglas Puddifoot/© Queen Productions Ltd; 43: Neal Preston/© Queen Productions Ltd; 45: Peter Still/Redferns/Getty Images; 50: Neal Preston/© Queen Productions Ltd; 55: Terence Spencer/The LIFE Images Collection/Getty Images; 59: Rob Verhorst/Redferns/Getty Images; 61: Richard Creamer/Michael Ochs Archives/Getty Images; 76: Neal Preston/© Queen Productions Ltd; 80: Neal Preston/© Queen Productions Ltd; 89 (centre left): © Queen Productions Ltd; 89 (bottom left): © Mercury Songs Ltd; 94: Neal Preston/© Queen Productions Ltd; 97: David Redfern/Redferns/Getty Images; 105: © Mercury Songs Ltd; 110: Simon Fowler/© Queen Productions Ltd; 113: Simon Fowler/© Queen Productions Ltd; 117 (top left): © Band Aid Trust; 117 (top right): Peter Still/Redferns/Getty Images; 120 (top left): © Band Aid Trust; 120 (bottom right): Design Richard Gray, Illustration Peter Blake/© Band Aid Trust; 139: Watal Asanuma/© Shinko Music; 140-158: © Queen Productions Ltd

Live Aid Logo(s) licensed courtesy of Band Aid Trust

Every effort has been made to acknowledge correctly and contact the source and/or copyright holder of each picture and Carlton Books Limited apologises for any unintentional errors or omissions, which will be corrected in future editions of this book.